Utopia Limited by Gilbert & Sullivan

Or, The Flowers of Progress

Libretto by William S. Gilbert
Music by Arthur Sullivan

The partnership between William Schwenck Gilbert and Arthur Seymour Sullivan and their canon of Savoy Operas is rightly lauded by all lovers of comic opera the world over.

Gilbert's sharp, funny words and Sullivan's deliciously lively and hummable tunes create a world that is distinctly British in view but has the world as its audience.

Both men were exceptionally talented and gifted in their own right and wrote much, often with other partners, that still stands the test of time. However, together as a team they created Light or Comic Operas of a standard that have had no rivals equal to their standard, before or since. That's quite an achievement.

To be recognised by the critics is one thing but their commercial success was incredible. The profits were astronomical, allowing for the building of their own purpose built theatre – The Savoy Theatre.

Beginning with the first of their fourteen collaborations, Thespis in 1871 and travelling through many classics including The Sorcerer (1877), H.M.S. Pinafore (1878), The Pirates of Penzance (1879), The Mikado (1885), The Gondoliers (1889) to their finale in 1896 with The Grand Duke, Gilbert & Sullivan created a legacy that is constantly revived and admired in theatres and other media to this very day.

Index of Contents

Utopia, Limited, or The Flowers of Progress was the thirteenth collaboration between Gilbert & Sullivan and premiered on October 7, 1893 at the Savoy Theatre and ran for 245 performances.

DRAMATIS PERSONAE
King Paramount, the First (King of Utopia)
Scaphio and Phantis (Judges of the Utopian Supreme Court)
Tarara (The Public Exploder)

Calynx (The Utopian Vice-Chamberlain)
Imported Flowers of Progress:

Lord Dramaleigh (a British Lord Chamberlain)
Captain Fitzbattleaxe (First Life Guards)
Captain Sir Edward Corcoran, K.C.B. (of the Royal Navy)
Mr. Goldbury (a company promoter; afterwards Comptroller of the Utopian Household)
Sir Bailey Barre, Q.C., M.P.
Mr. Blushington (of the County Council)

The Princess Zara (eldest daughter of King Paramount)
The Princesses Nekaya and Kalyba (her Younger Sisters)
The Lady Sophy (their English Gouvernante)

Utopian Maidens:
Salata
Melene
Phylla

SCENES
ACT I - A Utopian Palm Grove
ACT II - Throne Room in King Paramount's Palace

MUSICAL NUMBERS
Introduction
ACT I
1. In lazy languor motionless (Phylla and Chorus of Girls)
2. O make way for the Wise Men (Chorus)
2a. In every mental lore (Scaphio and Phantis)
3. Let all your doubts take wing (Scaphio and Phantis)
4. Quaff the nectar (Chorus)
4a. A King of autocratic power we (King with Chorus)
4b. Although of native maids the cream (Nekaya and Kalyba)
4c. Bold-faced ranger (Lady Sophy with Chorus)
5. First you're born (King with Scaphio and Phantis)
6. Subjected to your heavenly gaze (King and Lady Sophy)
7. Oh, maiden rich in Girton lore (Zara, Fitzbattleaxe., Troopers, and Chorus)
8. Ah! gallant soldier (Zara, Fitzbattleaxe., Troopers, and Chorus)
9. It's understood, I think (Zara, Fitzbattleaxe., Scaphio, and Phantis)
10. Oh, admirable art (Zara and Fitzbattleaxe.)
(11. Cut song for Zara, Youth is a boon avowed, (sung on the first night.)
12. Act I Finale: Although your Royal summons to appear (Ensemble) and When Britain sounds the trump of war (Zara, Sir Bailey Barre, and Chorus)
12a. What these may be" (Zara, Dramaleigh, Blushington, and Chorus) and A company promoter this (Zara, Goldbury, and Chorus)

12b. I'm Captain Corcoran, K.C.B. (Capt. Corcoran with Chorus) and Ye wand'rers from a mighty State (Quartet, Chorus, and Soli)

12c. Some seven men form an association (Mr Goldbury with Chorus), Well, at first sight it strikes us as dishonest (Ensemble), and Henceforward of a verity (King Paramount and Ensemble)

ACT II

13. Oh, Zara! and A tenor, all singers above (Fitzbattleaxe.)

14. Words of love too loudly spoken (Zara and Fitzbattleaxe.)

15. Society has quite forsaken (King with Chorus of Six Flowers of Progress)

16. Entrance of Court

17. Drawing Room Music

18.This ceremonial, Eagle high in cloudland soaring" (King and Ensemble)

19. With fury deep we burn" (Scaphio, Phantis, and King Paramount)

20. If you think that when banded in unity" (King, Scaphio and Phantis)

21. With wily brain (Scaphio, Phantis, and Tarara)

22. A wonderful joy our eyes to bless (Mr. Goldbury)

23. Then I may sing and play? (Nekaya, Kalyba, Lord D., and Mr Goldbury)

24. Oh, would some demon pow'r, When but a maid of fifteen year (Lady Sophy)

25. Ah, Lady Sophy, then you love me! (King and Lady Sophy)

25a. Oh, rapture unrestrained (King and Lady Sophy)

25b. Tarantella

26. "Upon our sea-girt land" (Chorus)

27. Finale Act II: "There's a little group of isles beyond the wave" (Zara, King Paramount, and Ensemble)

ACT I

OPENING CHORUS

In lazy languor—motionless,
We lie and dream of nothingness;
For visions come
From Poppydom
Direct at our command:
Or, delicate alternative,
In open idleness we live,
With lyre and lute
And silver flute,
The life of Lazyland.

SOLO—**PHYLLA**

The song of birds
In ivied towers;
The rippling play
Of waterway;
The lowing herds;
The breath of flowers;
The languid loves

Of turtle doves—
These simply joys are all at hand
Upon thy shores, O Lazyland!

(Enter CALYNX)

CALYNX
Good news! Great news! His Majesty's eldest daughter, Princess Zara, who left our shores five years since to go to England—the greatest, the most powerful, the wisest country in the world—has taken a high degree at Girton, and is on her way home again, having achieved a complete mastery over all the elements that have tended to raise that glorious country to her present pre-eminent position among Civilized nations!

SALATA
Then in a few months Utopia may hope to be completely Anglicized?

CALYNX
Absolutely and without a doubt.

MELENE (lazily)
We are very well as we are. Life without a care—every want supplied by a kind and fatherly monarch, who, despot though he be, has no other thought than to make his people happy—what have we to gain by the great change that is in store for us?

SALATA
What have we to gain? English institutions, English tastes, and oh, English fashions!

CALYNX
England has made herself what she is because, in that favored land, every one has to think for himself. Here we have no need to think, because our monarch anticipates all our wants, and our political opinions are formed for us by the journals to which we subscribe. Oh, think how much more brilliant this dialogue would have been, if we had been accustomed to exercise our reflective powers! They say that in England the conversation of the very meanest is a coruscation of impromptu epigram!

(Enter TARARA in a great rage)

TARARA
Lalabalele talala! Callabale lalabalica falahle!

CALYNX (horrified)
Stop—stop, I beg!

(All the LADIES close their ears.)

TARARA
Callamalala galalate! Caritalla lalabalee kallalale poo!

LADIES

Oh, stop him! stop him!

CALYNX

My lord, I'm surprised at you. Are you not aware that His Majesty, in his despotic acquiescence with the emphatic wish of his people, has ordered that the Utopian language shall be banished from his court, and that all communications shall henceforward be made in the English tongue?

TARARA

Yes, I'm perfectly aware of it, although—(suddenly presenting an explosive "cracker"). Stop—allow me.

CALYNX

(pulls it). Now, what's that for?

TARARA

Why, I've recently been appointed Public Exploder to His Majesty, and as I'm constitutionally nervous, I must accustom myself by degrees to the startling nature of my duties. Thank you. I was about to say that although, as Public Exploder, I am next in succession to the throne, I never the-less do my best to fall in with the royal decree. But when I am overmastered by an indignant sense of overwhelming wrong, as I am now, I slip into my native tongue without knowing it. I am told that in the language of that great and pure nation, strong expressions do not exist, consequently when I want to let off steam I have no alternative but to say, "Lalabalele molola lililah kallalale poo!"

CALYNX

But what is your grievance?

TARARA

This—by our Constitution we are governed by a Despot who, although in theory absolute—is, in practice, nothing of the kind—being watched day and night by two Wise Men whose duty it is, on his very first lapse from political or social propriety, to denounce him to me, the Public Exploder, and it then becomes my duty to blow up His Majesty with dynamite—allow me. (Presenting a cracker which CALYNX pulls.) Thank you—and, as some compensation to my wounded feelings, I reign in his stead.

CALYNX

Yes. After many unhappy experiments in the direction of an ideal Republic, it was found that what may be described as a Despotism tempered by Dynamite provides, on the whole, the most satisfactory description of ruler—an autocrat who dares not abuse his autocratic power.

TARARA

That's the theory—but in practice, how does it act?
Now, do you ever happen to see the Palace Peeper?

(Producing a "Society" paper).

CALYNX

Never even heard of the journal.

TARARA

I'm not surprised, because His Majesty's agents always buy up the whole edition; but I have an aunt in the publishing department, and she has supplied me with a copy. Well, it actually teems with circumstantially convincing details of the King's abominable immoralities! If this high-class journal may be believed, His Majesty is one of the most Heliogabalian profligates that ever disgraced an Autocratic throne! And do these Wise Men denounce him to me? Not a bit of it! They wink at his immoralities! Under the circumstances I really think I am justified in exclaiming "Lalabelele molola lililah kalabalale poo!" (All horrified.) I don't care—the occasion demands it.

(Exit TARARA)

(March. Enter GUARD, escorting SCAPHIO and PHANTIS)

CHORUS
O make way for the Wise Men!
They are the prizemen—
Double-first in the world's university!
For though lovely this island
(Which is my land),
She has no one to match them in her city.
They're the pride of Utopia—
Cornucopia
Is each his mental fertility.
O they make no blunder,
And no wonder,
For they're triumphs of infallibility.

DUET—**SCAPHIO and PHANTIS**
In every mental lore
(The statement smacks of vanity)
We claim to rank before
The wisest of humanity.
As gifts of head and heart
We wasted on "utility,"
We're "cast" to play a part
Of great responsibility.

Our duty is to spy
Upon our King's illicites,
And keep a watchful eye
On all his eccentricities.
If ever a trick he tries
That savours of rascality,
At our decree he dies
Without the least formality.

We fear no rude rebuff,
Or newspaper publicity;
Our word is quite enough,

The rest is electricity.
A pound of dynamite
Explodes in his auriculars;
It's not a pleasant sight—
We'll spare you the particulars.

Its force all men confess,
The King needs no admonishing—
We may say its success
Is something quite astonishing.
Our despot it imbues
With virtues quite delectable,
He minds his P's and Q's,—
And keeps himself respectable.

Of a tyrant polite
He's paragon quite.
He's as modest and mild
In his ways as a child;
And no one ever met
With an autocrat yet,
So delightfully bland
To the least in the land!

So make way for the wise men, etc.

(Exeunt all but SCAPHIO and PHANTIS. PHANTIS is pensive.)

SCAPHIO
Phantis, you are not in your customary exuberant spirits.
What is wrong?

PHANTIS
Scaphio, I think you once told me that you have never loved?

SCAPHIO
Never! I have often marvelled at the fairy influence which weaves its rosy web about the faculties of the greatest and wisest of our race; but I thank Heaven I have never been subjected to its singular fascination. For, oh, Phantis! there is that within me that tells me that when my time does come, the convulsion will be tremendous! When I love, it will be with the accumulated fervor of sixty-six years! But I have an ideal—a semi-transparent Being, filled with an inorganic pink jelly—and I have never yet seen the woman who approaches within measurable distance of it. All are opaque—opaque—opaque!

PHANTIS
Keep that ideal firmly before you, and love not until you find her. Though but fifty-five, I am an old campaigner in the battle-fields of Love; and, believe me, it is better to be as you are, heart-free and happy, than as I am—eternally racked with doubting agonies! Scaphio, the Princess Zara returns from England today!

SCAPHIO
My poor boy, I see it all.

PHANTIS
Oh! Scaphio, she is so beautiful. Ah! you smile, for you have never seen her. She sailed for England three months before you took office.

SCAPHIO
Now tell me, is your affection requited?

PHANTIS
I do not know—I am not sure. Sometimes I think it is, and then come these torturing doubts! I feel sure that she does not regard me with absolute indifference, for she could never look at me without having to go to bed with a sick headache.

SCAPHIO
That is surely something. Come, take heart, boy! You are
young and beautiful. What more could maiden want?

PHANTIS
Ah! Scaphio, remember she returns from a land where every youth is as a young Greek god, and where such beauty as I can boast is seen at every turn.

SCAPHIO
Be of good cheer! Marry her, boy, if so your fancy wills, and be sure that love will come.

PHANTIS (overjoyed)
Then you will assist me in this?

SCAPHIO
Why, surely! Silly one, what have you to fear? We have but to say the word, and her father must consent. Is he not our very slave? Come, take heart. I cannot bear to see you sad.

PHANTIS
Now I may hope, indeed! Scaphio, you have placed me on the very pinnacle of human joy!

DUET—**SCAPHIO and PHANTIS**

SCAPHIO
Let all your doubts take wing—
Our influence is great.
If Paramount our King
Presume to hesitate
Put on the screw,
And caution him
That he will rue
Disaster grim

That must ensue
To life and limb,
Should he pooh-pooh
This harmless whim.

BOTH
This harmless whim—this harmless whim,
It is as I/you say, a harmless whim.

PHANTIS (dancing)
Observe this dance
Which I employ
When I, by chance
Go mad with joy.
What sentiment
Does this express?

(PHANTIS continues his dance while SCAPHIO vainly endeavors to Discover its meaning)

Supreme content
And happiness!

BOTH
Of course it does! Of course it does!
Supreme content and happiness.

PHANTIS
Your friendly aid conferred,
I need no longer pine.
I've but to speak the word,
And lo, the maid is mine!
I do not choose
To be denied.
Or wish to lose
A lovely bride—
If to refuse
The King decide,
The royal shoes
Then woe betide!

BOTH
Then woe betide—then woe betide!
The Royal shoes then woe betide!

SCAPHIO
(Dancing) This step to use
I condescend
Whene'er I choose

To serve a friend.
What it implies
Now try to guess;

(SCAPHIO continues his dance while PHANTIS is vainly endeavouring to discover its meaning)

It typifies
Unselfishness!

BOTH
(Dancing) Of course it does! Of course it does!
It typifies unselfishness.

(Exeunt SCAPHIO and PHANTIS.)

March. Enter KING PARAMOUNT, attended by GUARDS and NOBLES, and preceded by GIRLS dancing
before him.

CHORUS
Quaff the nectar—cull the roses—
Gather fruit and flowers in plenty!
For our king no longer poses—
Sing the songs of far niente!
Wake the lute that sets us lilting,
Dance a welcome to each comer;
Day by day our year is wilting—
Sing the sunny songs of summer!
La, la, la, la!

SOLO—**KING**
A King of autocratic power we—
A despot whose tyrannic will is law—
Whose rule is paramount o'er land and sea,
A presence of unutterable awe!
But though the awe that I inspire
Must shrivel with imperial fire
All foes whom it may chance to touch,
To judge by what I see and hear,
It does not seem to interfere
With popular enjoyment, much.

CHORUS
No, no—it does not interfere
With our enjoyment much.

Stupendous when we rouse ourselves to strike,
Resistless when our tyrant thunder peals,
We often wonder what obstruction's like,

And how a contradicted monarch feels.
But as it is our Royal whim
Our Royal sails to set and trim
To suit whatever wind may blow—
What buffets contradiction deals
And how a thwarted monarch feels
We probably will never know.

CHORUS
No, no—what thwarted monarch feels,
You'll never, never know.

RECITATIVE—**KING**
My subjects all, it is your with emphatic
That all Utopia shall henceforth be modelled
Upon that glorious country called Great Britain—
To which some add—but others do not—Ireland.

CHORUS
It is!

KING
That being so, as you insist upon it,
We have arranged that our two younger daughters
Who have been "finished" by an English Lady—
(tenderly)   A grave and good and gracious English Lady—
Shall daily be exhibited in public,
That all may learn what, from the English standpoint,
Is looked upon as maidenly perfection!
Come hither, daughters!

(Enter NEKAYA and KALYBA. They are twins, about fifteen years old; they are very modest and demure in their appearance, dress and manner. They stand with their hands folded and their eyes cast down.)

CHORUS
How fair! how modest! how discreet!
How bashfully demure!
See how they blush, as they've been taught,
At this publicity unsought!
How English and how pure!

DUET—**NEKAYA and KALYBA**

BOTH
Although of native maids the cream,
We're brought up on the English scheme—
The best of all
For great and small

Who modesty adore.

NEKAYA

For English girls are good as gold,
Extremely modest (so we're told)
Demurely coy—divinely cold—
And that we are—and more.

KALYBA

To please papa, who argues thus—
All girls should mould themselves on us
Because we are
By furlongs far
The best of the bunch,
We show ourselves to loud applause
From ten to four without a pause—

NEKAYA

Which is an awkward time because
It cuts into our lunch.

BOTH

Oh maids of high and low degree,
Whose social code is rather free,
Please look at us and you will see
What good young ladies ought to be!

NEKAYA

And as we stand, like clockwork toys,
A lecturer whom papa employs
Proceeds to prussia
Our modest ways
And guileless character—

KALYBA

Our well-known blush—our downcast eyes—
Our famous look of mild surprise.

NEKAYA

(Which competition still defies)—
Our celebrated "Sir!!!"

KALYBA

Then all the crowd take down our looks
In pocket memorandum books.
To diagnose
Our modest pose
The Kodaks do their best:

NEKAYA
If evidence you would possess
Of what is maiden bashfulness
You need only a button press—

KALYBA
And we will do the rest.

Enter LADY SOPHY—an English lady of mature years and extreme Gravity of demeanour and dress.
She carries a lecturer's wand in her hand. She is led on by the KING, who expresses great regard and
admiration for her.

RECITATIVE—**LADY SOPHY**
This morning we propose to illustrate
A course of maiden courtship, from the start
To the triumphant matrimonial finish.

(Through the following song the two PRINCESSES illustrate in Gesture the description given by LADY
SOPHY.)

SONG—**LADY SOPHY**
Bold-faced ranger
(Perfect stranger)
Meets two well-behaved young ladies.
He's attractive,
Young and active—
Each a little bit afraid is.
Youth advances,
At his glances
To their danger they awaken;
They repel him
As they tell him
He is very much mistaken.
Though they speak to him politely,
Please observe they're sneering slightly,
Just to show he's acting vainly.
This is Virtue saying plainly
"Go away, young bachelor,
We are not what you take us for!"
When addressed impertinently,
English ladies answer gently,
"Go away, young bachelor,
We are not what you take us for!"

As he gazes,
Hat he raises,
Enters into conversation.

Makes excuses—
This produces
Interesting agitation.
He, with daring,
Undespairing,
Give his card—his rank discloses
Little heeding
This proceeding,
They turn up their little noses.
Pray observe this lesson vital—
When a man of rank and title
His position first discloses,
Always cock your little noses.
When at home, let all the class
Try this in the looking glass.
English girls of well bred notions,
Shun all unrehearsed emotions.
English girls of highest class
Practice them before the glass.

His intentions
Then he mentions.
Something definite to go on—
Makes recitals
Of his titles,
Hints at settlements, and so on.
Smiling sweetly,
They, discreetly,
Ask for further evidences:
Thus invited,
He, delighted,
Gives the usual references:
This is business. Each is fluttered
When the offer's fairly uttered.
"Which of them has his affection?"
He declines to make selection.
Do they quarrel for his dross?
Not a bit of it—they toss!
Please observe this cogent moral—
English ladies never quarrel.
When a doubt they come across,
English ladies always toss.

RECITATIVE—**LADY SOPHY**
The lecture's ended. In ten minute's space
'Twill be repeated in the market-place!

(Exit LADY SOPHY, followed by NEKAYA and KALYBA.)

CHORUS
Quaff the nectar—cull the roses—
Bashful girls will soon be plenty!
Maid who thus at fifteen poses
Ought to be divine at twenty!

(Exeunt all but KING.)

KING
I requested Scaphio and Phantis to be so good as to favor
Me with an audience this morning.

(Enter SCAPHIO and PHANTIS.)

Oh, here they are!

SCAPHIO
Your Majesty wished to speak with us, I believe. You—you needn't keep your crown on, on our account, you know.

KING
I beg your pardon. (Removes it.) I always forget that! Odd, the notion of a King not being allowed to wear one of his own crowns in the presence of two of his own subjects.

PHANTIS
Yes—bizarre, is it not?

KING
Most quaint. But then it's a quaint world.

PHANTIS
Teems with quiet fun. I often think what a lucky thing
It is that you are blessed with such a keen sense of humor!

KING
Do you know, I find it invaluable. Do what I will, I cannot help looking at the humorous side of things—for, properly considered, everything has its humorous side—even the Palace Peeper (producing it). See here—"Another Royal Scandal," by Junius Junior. "How long is this to last?" by Senex Senior. "Ribald Royalty," by Mercury Major. "Where is the Public Exploder?" by Mephistopheles Minor. When I reflect that all these outrageous attacks on my morality are written by me, at your command—well, it's one of the funniest things that have come within the scope of my experience.

SCAPHIO
Besides, apart from that, they have a quiet humor of their own which is simply irresistible.

KING (gratified)

Not bad, I think. Biting, trenchant sarcasm—the rapier, not the bludgeon—that's my line. But then it's so easy—I'm such a good subject—a bad King but a good Subject—ha! ha!—a capital heading for next week's leading article! (makes a note) And then the stinging little paragraphs about our Royal goings-on with our Royal Second Housemaid—delicately sub-acid, are they not?

SCAPHIO
My dear King, in that kind of thing no one can hold a candle to you.

PHANTIS
But the crowning joke is the Comic Opera you've written
For us—"King Tuppence, or A Good Deal Less than Half a
Sovereign"—in which the celebrated English tenor, Mr.
Wilkinson, burlesques your personal appearance and gives grotesque
imitations of your Royal peculiarities. It's immense!

KING
Ye—es—That's what I wanted to speak to you about. Now I've not the least doubt but that even that has its Humorous side too—if one could only see it. As a rule I'm pretty quick at detecting latent humor—but I confess I do not quite see where it comes in, in this particular instance. It's so horribly personal!

SCAPHIO
Personal? Yes, of course it's personal—but consider the antithetical humor of the situation.

KING
Yes. I—I don't think I've quite grasped that.

SCAPHIO
No? You surprise me. Why, consider. During the day thousands tremble at your frown, during the night (from 8 to 11) thousands roar at it. During the day your most arbitrary pronouncements are received by your subjects with abject submission—during the night, they shout with joy at your most terrible decrees. It's not every monarch who enjoys the privilege of undoing by night all the despotic absurdities he's committed during the day.

KING
Of course! Now I see it! Thank you very much. I was sure it had its humorous side, and it was very dull of me not to have seen it before. But, as I said just now, it's a quaint world.

PHANTIS
Teems with quiet fun.

KING
Yes. Properly considered, what a farce life is, to be sure!

SONG—**KING**
First you're born—and I'll be bound you
Find a dozen strangers round you.
"Hallo," cries the new-born baby,

"Where's my parents? which may they be?"
Awkward silence—no reply—
Puzzled baby wonders why!
Father rises, bows politely—
Mother smiles (but not too brightly)—
Doctor mumbles like a dumb thing—
Nurse is busy mixing something.—
Every symptom tends to show
You're decidedly de trop—

ALL

Ho! ho! ho! ho! ho! ho! ho! ho!
Time's teetotum,
If you spin it,
Gives it quotum
Once a minute.
I'll go bail
You hit the nail,
And if you fail,
The deuce is in it!

KING

You grow up and you discover
What it is to be a lover.
Some young lady is selected—
Poor, perhaps, but well-connected.
Whom you hail (for Love is blind)
As the Queen of fairy kind.
Though she's plain—perhaps unsightly,
Makes her face up—laces tightly,
In her form your fancy traces
All the gifts of all the graces.
Rivals none the maiden woo,
So you take her and she takes you.

ALL

Ho! ho! ho! ho! ho! ho! ho! ho!
Joke beginning,
Never ceases
Till your inning
Time releases,
On your way
You blindly stray,
And day by day
The joke increases!

KING
Ten years later—Time progresses—

Sours your temper—thins your tresses;
Fancy, then, her chain relaxes;
Rates are facts and so are taxes.
Fairy Queen's no longer young—
Fairy Queen has got a tongue.
Twins have probably intruded—
Quite unbidden—just as you did—
They're a source of care and trouble—
Just as you were—only double.
Comes at last the final stroke—
Time has had its little joke!

ALL
Ho! ho! ho! ho! ho! ho! ho! ho!
Daily driven
(Wife as drover)
Ill you've thriven—
Ne'er in clover;
Lastly, when
Three-score and ten
(And not till then),
The joke is over!
Ho! ho! ho! ho! ho! ho! ho! ho!
Then—and then
The joke is over!

(Exeunt SCAPHIO and PHANTIS)

KING
(putting on his crown again) It's all very well. I always like to look on the humorous side of things; but I do not think I ought to be required to write libels on my own moral character. Naturally, I see the joke of it—anybody would—but Zara's coming home today; she's no longer a child, and I confess I should not like her to see my Opera—though it's uncommonly well written; and I should be sorry if the Palace Peeper got into her hands—though It's certainly smart—very smart indeed. It is almost a pity that I have to buy up the whole edition, because it's really too good to be lost. And Lady Sophy—that blameless type of perfect womanhood! Great Heavens, what would she say if the Second Housemaid business happened to meet her pure blue eye!

(Enter LADY SOPHY)

LADY SOPHY
My monarch is soliloquizing. I will withdraw. (going)

KING
No—pray don't go. Now I'll give you fifty chances, and
You won't guess whom I was thinking of.

LADY SOPHY

Alas, sir, I know too well. Ah! King, it's an old, old story, and I'm well nigh weary of it! Be warned in time—from my heart I pity you, but I am not for you!

(going)

KING
But hear what I have to say.

LADY SOPHY
It is useless. Listen. In the course of a long and adventurous career in the principal European Courts, it has been revealed to me that I unconsciously exercise a weird and supernatural fascination over all Crowned Heads. So irresistible is this singular property, that there is not a European Monarch who has not implored me, with tears in His eyes, to quit his kingdom, and take my fatal charms elsewhere. As time was getting on it occurred to me that by descending several pegs in the scale of Respectability I might qualify your Majesty for my hand. Actuated by this humane motive and happening to possess Respectability enough for Six, I consented to confer Respectability enough for Four upon your two younger daughters—but although I have, alas, only Respectability enough for Two left, there is still, as I gather from the public press of this country (producing the Palace Peeper), a considerable balance in My favor.

KING (aside)
Damn! (aloud) May I ask how you came by this?

LADY SOPHY
It was handed to me by the officer who holds the position
Of Public Exploder to your Imperial Majesty.

KING
And surely, Lady Sophy, surely you are not so unjust as
To place any faith in the irresponsible gabble of the
Society press!

LADY SOPHY (referring to paper)
I read on the authority of Senex
Senior that your Majesty was seen dancing with your
Second Housemaid on the Oriental Platform of the Tivoli Gardens.
That is untrue?

KING
Absolutely. Our Second Housemaid has only one leg.

LADY SOPHY (suspiciously)
How do you know that?

KING
Common report. I give you my honor.

LADY SOPHY

It may be so. I further read—and the statement is vouched for by no less an authority that Mephistopheles Minor—that your Majesty indulges in a bath of hot rum-punch every morning. I trust I do not lay myself open to the charge of displaying an indelicate curiosity as to the mysteries of the royal dressing-room when I ask if there is any foundation for this statement?

KING
None whatever. When our medical adviser exhibits rum-punch it is as a draught, not as a fomentation. As to our bath, our valet plays the garden hose upon us every morning.

LADY SOPHY (shocked)
Oh, pray—pray spare me these unseemly details. Well, you are a Despot—have you taken steps to slay this scribbler?

KING
Well, no—I have not gone so far as that. After all, it's the poor devil's living, you know.

LADY SOPHY
It is the poor devil's living that surprises me. If this man lies, there is no recognized punishment that is sufficiently terrible for him.

KING
That's precisely it. I—I am waiting until a punishment
Is discovered that will exactly meet the enormity of the case.
I am in constant communication with the Mikado of Japan,
Who is a leading authority on such points; and, moreover, I
Have the ground plans and sectional elevations of several
Capital punishments in my desk at this moment. Oh, Lady Sophy,
As you are powerful, be merciful!

DUET—**KING and LADY SOPHY**

KING
Subjected to your heavenly gaze
(Poetical phrase),
My brain is turned completely.
Observe me now
No monarch I vow,
Was ever so afflicted!

LADY SOPHY
I'm pleased with that poetical phrase,
"A heavenly gaze,"
But though you put it neatly,
Say what you will,
These paragraphs still
Remain uncontradicted.

Come, crush me this contemptible worm

(A forcible term),
If he's assailed you wrongly.
The rage display,
Which, as you say,
Has moved your Majesty lately.

KING
Though I admit that forcible term
"Contemptible worm,"
Appeals to me most strongly,
To treat this pest
As you suggest
Would pain my Majesty greatly.

LADY SOPHY
This writer lies!

KING
Yes, bother his eyes!

LADY SOPHY
He lives, you say?

KING
In a sort of way.

LADY SOPHY
Then have him shot.

KING
Decidedly not.

LADY SOPHY
Or crush him flat.

KING
I cannot do that.

BOTH
O royal Rex,

My/her blameless sex
Abhors such conduct shady.
You/I plead in vain,
I/you will never gain
Respectable English lady!

(Dance of repudiation by LADY SOPHY. Exit followed by KING.)

March. Enter all the Court, heralding the arrival of the PRINCESS ZARA, who enters, escorted by
CAPTAIN FITZBATTLEAXE and four Troopers, all in the full uniform of the First Life Guards.

CHORUS
Oh, maiden, rich
In Girton lore
That wisdom which,
We prized before,
We do confess
Is nothingness,
And rather less,
Perhaps, than more.
On each of us
Thy learning shed.
On calculus
May we be fed.
And teach us, please,
To speak with ease,
All languages,
Alive and dead!

SOLO—**PRINCESS and CHORUS**

ZARA
Five years have flown since I took wing—
Time flies, and his footstep ne'er retards—
I'm the eldest daughter of your King.

TROOP
And we are her escort—First Life Guards!
On the royal yacht,
When the waves were white,
In a helmet hot
And a tunic tight,
And our great big boots,
We defied the storm;
For we're not recruits,
And his uniform
A well drilled trooper ne'er discards—
And we are her escort—First Life Guards!

ZARA
These gentlemen I present to you,
The pride and boast of their barrack-yards;
They've taken, O! such care of me!

TROOP

For we are her escort—First Life Guards!
When the tempest rose,
And the ship went so—
Do you suppose
We were ill? No, no!
Though a qualmish lot
In a tunic tight,
And a helmet hot,
And a breastplate bright
(Which a well-drilled trooper ne'er discards),
We stood as her escort—First Life Guards!

CHORUS
Knightsbridge nursemaids—serving fairies—
Stars of proud Belgravian airies;
At stern duty's call you leave them,
Though you know how that must grieve them!

ZARA
Tantantarara-rara-rara!

FITZBATTLEAXE
Trumpet-call of Princess Zara!

CHORUS
That's trump-call, and they're all trump cards—
They are her escort—First Life Guards!

ENSEMBLE

CHORUS, PRINCESS ZARA and FITZBATTLEAXE

LADIES
Oh! the hours are gold,
And the joys untold,
Knightsbridge nursemaids, etc.
When my eyes behold
My beloved Princess;

MEN
And the years will seem
When the tempest rose, etc.
But a brief day-dream,
In the joy extreme
Of our happiness!

Full CHORUS Knightsbridge nursemaids, serving fairies, etc.

(Enter KING, PRINCESS NEKAYA and KALYBA, and LADY SOPHY. As the KING enters, the escort present arms.)

KING
Zara! my beloved daughter! Why, how well you look and How lovely you have grown!

(Embraces her.)

ZARA
My dear father! (embracing him) And my two beautiful little sisters! (embracing them)

NEKAYA
Not beautiful.

KALYBA
Nice-looking.

ZARA
But first let me present to you the English warrior who commands my escort, and who has taken, O! such care of me during my voyage—Captain Fitzbattleaxe!

TROOPERS
The First Life Guards.
When the tempest rose,
And the ship went so—

(CAPTAIN FITZBATTLE motions them to be silent. The Troopers place themselves in the four corners of the stage, standing at ease, immovably, as if on sentry. Each is surrounded by an admiring group of young LADIES, of whom they take no notice.)

KING (to CAPTAIN BATTLEAXE)
Sir, you come from a country where every virtue flourishes. We trust that you will not criticize too severely such shortcomings as you may detect in our semi-barbarous society.

FITZBATTLEAXE (looking at ZARA)
Sir, I have eyes for nothing but the blameless and the beautiful.

KING
We thank you—he is really very polite! (Lady Sophy, who
Has been greatly scandalized by the attentions paid to the
Life guardsmen by the young ladies, marches the Princesses
Nekaya and Kalyba towards an exit.) Lady Sophy, do not leave us.

LADY SOPHY
Sir, your children are young, and, so far, innocent. If they are to remain so, it is necessary that they be at once removed from the contamination of their present disgraceful surroundings. (She marches them off.)

KING (whose attention has thus been called to the proceedings of the young ladies—aside)
Dear, dear! They really shouldn't. (Aloud) Captain Fitzbattleaxe—

FITZBATTLEAXE
Sir.

KING
Your Troopers appear to be receiving a troublesome amount
Of attention from those young ladies. I know how strict you
English soldiers are, and I should be extremely
Distressed if anything occurred to shock their puritanical British sensitiveness.

FITZBATTLEAXE
Oh, I don't think there's any chance of that.

KING
You think not? They won't be offended?

FITZBATTLEAXE
Oh no! They are quite hardened to it. They get a good deal of that sort of thing, standing sentry at the Horse Guards.

KING
It's English, is it?

FITZBATTLEAXE
It's particularly English.

KING
Then, of course, it's all right. Pray proceed, ladies, it's particularly English. Come, my daughter, for we have much to say to each other.

ZARA
Farewell, Captain Fitzbattleaxe! I cannot thank you too emphatically for the devoted care with which you have watched over me during our long and eventful voyage.

DUET—**ZARA and CAPTAIN BATTLEAXE**

ZARA
Ah! gallant soldier, brave and true
In tented field and tourney,
I grieve to have occasioned you
So very long a journey.
A British warrior give up all—
His home and island beauty—
When summoned to the trumpet call
Of Regimental Duty!

CHORUS
Tantantara-rara-rara!
Trumpet call of the Princess Zara!

ENSEMBLE

MEN
A British warrior gives up all, etc.
My delight to hide,
Ladies
Let us whisper low
Knightsbridge nursemaids, etc.
Lest the truth we show
We would fain conceal.

FITZBATTLEAXE and ZARA (aside)
Oh my joy, my pride,
Let us sing, aside,
What in truth we feel,

Of our love's glad glow,

FITZBATTLEAXE
Such escort duty, as his due,
To young Lifeguardsman falling
Completely reconciles him to
His uneventful calling.
When soldier seeks Utopian glades
In charge of Youth and Beauty,
Then pleasure merely masquerades
As Regimental Duty!

ALL
Tantantarara-rara-rara!
Trumpet-call of Princess Zara!

ENSEMBLE

MEN
A British warrior gives up all, etc.
And the joys untold,
When my eyes behold
Ladies
And the years will seem
Knightsbridge nursemaids, etc.
In the job extreme
Of our happiness!

FITZBATTLEAXE and ZARA (aside)
Oh! my hours are gold,

My beloved Princess;

But a brief day-dream,

(Exeunt KING and ZARA in one direction, Lifeguardsmen and crowd in opposite direction. Enter, at back, SCAPHIO and PHANTIS, who watch ZARA as she goes off. SCAPTIO is seated, shaking violently, and obviously under the influence of some strong emotion.)

PHANTIS
There—tell me, Scaphio, is she not beautiful? Can you wonder that I love her so passionately?

SCAPHIO

No. She is extraordinarily—miraculously lovely! Good heavens, what a singularly beautiful girl!

PHANTIS

I knew you would say so!

SCAPHIO

What exquisite charm of manner! What surprising delicacy
Of gesture! Why, she's a goddess! a very goddess!

PHANTIS (rather taken aback)

Yes—she's—she's an attractive girl.

SCAPHIO

Attractive? Why, you must be blind!—She's entrancing—enthralling—intoxicating! (Aside) God
bless my heart, what's the matter with me?

PHANTIS (alarmed)

Yes. You—you promised to help me to get her father's consent, you know.

SCAPHIO

Promised! Yes, but the convulsion has come, my good boy!
It is she—my ideal! Why, what's this? (Staggering)
Phantis! Stop me—I'm going mad—mad with the love of her!

PHANTIS

Scaphio, compose yourself, I beg. The girl is perfectly opaque! Besides, remember—each of us is
helpless without the other. You can't succeed without my consent, you know.

SCAPHIO

And you dare to threaten? Oh, ungrateful! When you came to me, palsied with love for this girl, and
implored my assistance, did I not unhesitatingly promise it? And this is the return you make? Out of my
sight, ingrate! (Aside) Dear! dear! what is the matter with me?

(Enter CAPTAIN FITZBATTLEAXE and ZARA)

ZARA

Dear me. I'm afraid we are interrupting a tete-a-tete.

SCAPHIO (breathlessly)

No, no. You come very appropriately. To be brief, we—we love you—this man and I—madly—
passionately!

ZARA

Sir!

SCAPHIO

And we don't know how we are to settle which of us is to marry you.

FITZBATTLEAXE
Zara, this is very awkward.

SCAPHIO (very much overcome)
I—I am paralyzed by the singular radiance of your extraordinary loveliness. I know I am incoherent. I never was like this before—it shall not occur again. I—shall be fluent, presently.

ZARA (aside)
Oh, dear, Captain Fitzbattleaxe, what is to be done?

FITZBATTLEAXE (aside)
Leave it to me—I'll manage it. (Aloud) It's a common situation. Why not settle it in the English fashion?

BOTH
The English fashion? What is that?

FITZBATTLEAXE
It's very simple. In England, when two gentlemen are in love with the same lady, and until it is settled which gentleman is to blow out the brains of the other, it is provided, by the Rival Admirers' Clauses Consolidation Act, that the lady shall be entrusted to an officer of Household Cavalry as stakeholder, who is bound to hand her over to the survivor (on the Tontine principle) in a good condition of substantial and decorative repair.

SCAPHIO
Reasonable wear and tear and damages by fire excepted?

FITZBATTLEAXE
Exactly.

PHANTIS
Well, that seems very reasonable. (To SCAPHIO) What do you say—Shall we entrust her to this officer of Household Cavalry? It will give us time.

SCAPHIO (trembling violently)
I—I am not at present in a condition to think it out coolly—but if he is an officer of Household Cavalry, and if the Princess consents—

ZARA
Alas, dear sirs, I have no alternative—under the Rival Admirers' Clauses Consolidation Act!

FITZBATTLEAXE
Good—then that's settled.

QUARTET—**FITZBATTLEAXE, ZARA, SCAPHIO, and PHANTIS.**

FITZBATTLEAXE

It's understood, I think, all round
That, by the English custom bound
I hold the lady safe and sound
In trust for either rival,
Until you clearly testify
By sword and pistol, by and by,
Which gentleman prefers to die,
And which prefers survival.

ENSEMBLE

SCAPHIO and PHANTIS

Its clearly understood all round
That, by your English custom bound
He holds the lady safe and sound
In trust for either rival,
Until we clearly testify
By sword or pistol, by and by
Which gentleman prefers to die,
Which prefers survival.

ZARA and FITZBATTLEAXE

We stand, I think, on safish ground
Our senses weak it will astound
If either gentleman is found
Prepared to meet his rival.
Their machinations we defy;
We won't be parted, you and I—
Of bloodshed each is rather shy—
They both prefer survival

PHANTIS

If I should die and he should live
(aside to FITZBATTLEAXE)
To you, without reserve, I give
Her heart so young and sensitive,
And all her predilections.

SCAPHIO

If he should live and I should die,
(aside to FITZBATTLEAXE)
I see no kind of reason why
You should not, if you wish it, try
To gain her young affections.

ENSEMBLE

SCAPHIO and PHANTIS

If I should die and you should live
To this young officer I give
Her heart so soft and sensitive,
And all her predilections.
If you should live and I should die
I see no kind of reason why
He should not, if he chooses, try
To win her young affections.

FITZBATTLEAXE and ZARA

As both of us are positive
That both of them intend to live,
There's nothing in the case to give
Us cause for grave reflections.
As both will live and neither die
I see no kind of reason why
I should not, if I wish it, try
To gain your young affections!

(Exit SCAPHIO and PHANTIS together)

DUET—**ZARA and FITZBATTLEAXE**

ENSEMBLE
Oh admirable art!
Oh, neatly-planned intention!
Oh, happy intervention—
Oh, well constructed plot!

When sages try to part
Two loving hearts in fusion,
Their wisdom's delusion,
And learning serves them not!

FITZBATTLEAXE
Until quit plain
Is their intent,
These sages twain
I represent.
Now please infer
That, nothing loth,
You're henceforth, as it were,
Engaged to marry both—
Then take it that I represent the two—
On that hypothesis, what would you do?

ZARA (aside)
What would I do? what would I do?
(To FITZBATTLEAXE)
In such a case,
Upon your breast,
My blushing face
I think I'd rest—(doing so)
Then perhaps I might
Demurely say—
"I find this breastplate bright
Is sorely in the way!"

FITZBATTLEAXE
Our mortal race
Is never blest—
There's no such case
As perfect rest;
Some petty blight
Asserts its sway—
Some crumbled roseleaf light
Is always in the way!

(Exit FITZBATTLEAXE. Manet ZARA.)

(Enter KING)

KING
My daughter! At last we are alone together.

ZARA
Yes, and I'm glad we are, for I want to speak to you very
seriously. Do you know this paper?

KING (aside)
Da—!
(Aloud) Oh yes—I've—I've seen it.
Where in the world did you get this from?

ZARA
It was given to me by Lady Sophy—my sisters' governess.

KING (aside)
Lady Sophy's an angel, but I do sometimes wish
she'd mind her own business!
(Aloud) It's—ha! ha!—it's
rather humorous.

ZARA
I see nothing humorous in it. I only see that you, the despotic King of this country, are made the subject
of the most scandalous insinuations. Why do you permit these things?

KING
Well, they appeal to my sense of humor. It's the only really comic paper in Utopia, and I wouldn't be
without it for the world.

ZARA
If it had any literary merit I could understand it.

KING
Oh, it has literary merit. Oh, distinctly, it has
Literary merit.

ZARA
My dear father, it's mere ungrammatical twaddle.

KING
Oh, it's not ungrammatical. I can't allow that.
Unpleasantly personal, perhaps, but written with an
Epigrammatical point that is very rare nowadays—very rare indeed.

ZARA (looking at cartoon)
Why do they represent you with such
A big nose?

KING (looking at cartoon)
Eh? Yes, it is a big one! Why,
The fact is that, in the cartoons of a comic paper, the size
Of your nose always varies inversely as the square of your popularity. It's the rule.

ZARA
Then you must be at a tremendous discount just now! I see a notice of a new piece called "King Tuppence," in which an English tenor has the audacity to personate you on a Public stage. I can only say that I am surprised that any English tenor should lend himself to such degrading personalities.

KING
Oh, he's not really English. As it happens he's a Utopian, but he calls himself English.

ZARA
Calls himself English?

KING
Yes. Bless you, they wouldn't listen to any tenor who didn't call himself English.

ZARA
And you permit this insolent buffoon to caricature you in a pointless burlesque! My dear father—if you were a free agent, you would never permit these outrages.

KING (almost in tears)
Zara—I—I admit I am not altogether a free agent. I—I am controlled. I try to make the best of it, but sometimes I find it very difficult—very difficult indeed. Nominally a Despot, I am, between ourselves, the helpless tool of two unscrupulous Wise Men, who insist on my falling in with all their wishes and threaten to denounce me for immediate explosion if I remonstrate!

(Breaks down completely)

ZARA
My poor father! Now listen to me. With a view to remodelling the political and social institutions of Utopia, I have brought with me six Representatives of the principal causes that have tended to make England the powerful, happy, and blameless country which the consensus of European civilization has declared it to be. Place yourself unreservedly in the hands of these gentlemen, and they will reorganize your country on a footing that will enable you to defy your persecutors. They are all now washing their hands after their journey. Shall I introduce them?

KING
My dear Zara, how can I thank you? I will consent to anything that will release me from the abominable tyranny of these two men.

(Calling)

What ho! Without there!

(Enter CALYNX)

Summon my Court without an instant's delay!

(Exit CALYNX)

FINALE
Enter every one, except the Flowers of Progress.

CHORUS
Although your Royal summons to appear
From courtesy was singularly free,
Obedient to that summons we are here—
What would your Majesty?

RECITATIVE—**KING**
My worthy people, my beloved daughter
Most thoughtfully has brought with her from England
The types of all the causes that have made
That great and glorious country what it is.

CHORUS
Oh, joy unbounded!

SCAPHIO, TARARA, PHANTIS (aside).
Why, what does this mean?

RECITATIVE—**ZARA**
Attend to me, Utopian populace,
Ye South Pacific island viviparians;
All, in the abstract, types of courtly grace,
Yet, when compared with Britain's glorious race,
But little better than half clothed Barbarians!

CHORUS
Yes! Contrasted when
With Englishmen,
Are little better than half-clothed barbarians!

Enter all the FLOWERS OF PROGRESS, led by FITZBATTLEAXE.

SOLOS—ZARA and the FLOWERS OF PROGRESS

(Presenting CAPTAIN FITZBATTLEAXE)

When Britain sounds the trump of war
(And Europe trembles),
The army of the conqueror
In serried ranks assemble;
'Tis then this warrior's eyes and sabre gleam
For our protection—
He represents a military scheme
In all its proud perfection!

CHORUS
Yes—yes
He represents a military scheme
In all its proud perfection.
Ulahlica! Ulahlica! Ulahlica!

SOLO—ZARA.

(Presenting SIR BAILEY BARRE, Q.C., M.P.)

A complicated gentleman allow to present,
Of all the arts and faculties the terse embodiment,
He's a great arithmetician who can demonstrate with ease
That two and two are three or five or anything you please;
An eminent Logician who can make it clear to you
That black is white—when looked at from the proper point
Of view;
A marvelous Philologist who'll undertake to show
That "yes" is but another and a neater form of "no."

SIR BAILEY
Yes—yes—yes—
"Yes" is but another and a neater form of "no."
All preconceived ideas on any subject I can scout,
And demonstrate beyond all possibility of doubt,
That whether you're an honest man or whether you're a thief
Depends on whose solicitor has given me my brief.

CHORUS
Yes—yes—yes
That whether your'e an honest man, etc.
Ulahlica! Ulahlica! Ulahlica!

ZARA
(Presenting Lord Dramaleigh and County Councillor)
What these may be, Utopians all,
Perhaps you'll hardly guess—
They're types of England's physical

And moral cleanliness.
This is a Lord High Chamberlain,
Of purity the gauge—
He'll cleanse our court from moral stain
And purify our Stage.

LORD DRAMALEIGH
Yes—yes—yes
Court reputations I revise,
And presentations scrutinize,
New plays I read with jealous eyes,
And purify the Stage.

CHORUS
Court reputations, etc.

ZARA
This County Councillor acclaim,
Great Britain's latest toy—
On anything you like to name
His talents he'll employ—

All streets and squares he'll purify
Within your city walls,
And keep meanwhile a modest eye
On wicked music halls.

COUNTY COUNCILLOR
Yes—yes—yes
In towns I make improvements great,
Which go to swell the County Rate—
I dwelling-houses sanitate,
And purify the Halls!

CHORUS
In towns he makes improvements great, etc.
Ulahlica! Ulahlica! Ulahlica!

SOLO—**ZARA**

(Presenting MR GOLDBURY)

A Company Promoter this with special education,
Which teaches what Contango means and also Backwardation—
To speculators he supplies a grand financial leaven,
Time was when two were company—but now it must be seven.

MR GOLDBURY

Yes—yes—yes
Stupendous loans to foreign thrones
I've largely advocated;
In ginger-pops and peppermint-drops
I've freely speculated;
Then mines of gold, of wealth untold,
Successfully I've floated
And sudden falls in apple-stalls
Occasionally quoted.
And soon or late I always call
For Stock Exchange quotation—
No schemes too great and none too small
For Companification!

CHORUS
Yes! Yes! Yes! No schemes too great, etc.
Ulahlica! Ulahlica! Ulahlica!

ZARA

(Presenting CAPTAIN SIR EDWARD CORCORAN, R.N.)

And lastly I present
Great Britain's proudest boast,
Who from the blows
Of foreign foes
Protects her sea-girt coast—
And if you ask him in respectful tone,
He'll show you how you may protect your own!

SOLO—**CAPTAIN CORCORAN**
I'm Captain Corcoran, K.C.B.,
I'll teach you how we rule the sea,
And terrify the simple Gauls;
And how the Saxon and the Celt
Their Europe-shaking blows have dealt
With Maxim gun and Nordenfelt
(Or will when the occasion calls).
If sailor-like you'd play your cards,
Unbend your sails and lower your yards,
Unstep your masts—you'll never want 'em more.
Though we're no longer hearts of oak,
Yet we can steer and we can stoke,
And thanks to coal, and thanks to coke,
We never run a ship ashore!

ALL
What never?

CAPTIN CORCORAN
No, never!

ALL
What never?

CAPTIN CORCORAN
Hardly ever!

ALL
Hardly ever run a ship ashore!
Then give three cheers, and three cheers more,
For the tar who never runs his ship ashore;
Then give three cheers, and three cheers more,
For he never runs his ship ashore!

CHORUS
All hail, ye types of England's power—
Ye heaven-enlightened band!
We bless the day and bless the hour
That brought you to our land.

QUARTET
Ye wanderers from a mighty State,
Oh, teach us how to legislate—
Your lightest word will carry weight,
In our attentive ears.
Oh, teach the natives of this land
(Who are not quick to understand)
How to work off their social and
Political arrears!

FITZBATTLEAXE
Increase your army!

LORD DRAMALEIGH
Purify your court!

CAPTIN CORCORAN
Get up your steam and cut your canvas short!

SIR BAILEY
To speak on both sides teach your sluggish brains!

MR BLUSHINGHAM
Widen your thoroughfares, and flush your drains!

MR GOLDBURY
Utopia's much too big for one small head—
I'll float it as a Company Limited!

KING
A Company Limited? What may that be?
The term, I rather think, is new to me.

CHORUS
A company limited? etc.

SCAPHIO, PHANTIS, TARARA (Aside)
What does he mean? What does he mean?
Give us a kind of clue!
What does he mean? What does he mean?
What is he going to do?

SONG—**MR GOLDBURY**
Some seven men form an Association
(If possible, all Peers and Baronets),
The start off with a public declaration
To what extent they mean to pay their debts.
That's called their Capital; if they are wary
They will not quote it at a sum immense.
The figure's immaterial—it may vary
From eighteen million down to eighteen pence.
I should put it rather low;
The good sense of doing so
Will be evident at once to any debtor.
When it's left to you to say
What amount you mean to pay,
Why, the lower you can put it at, the better.

CHORUS
When it's left to you to say, etc.

They then proceed to trade with all who'll trust 'em
Quite irrespective of their capital
(It's shady, but it's sanctified by custom);
Bank, Railway, Loan, or Panama Canal.
You can't embark on trading too tremendous—
It's strictly fair, and based on common sense—
If you succeed, your profits are stupendous—
And if you fail, pop goes your eighteenpence.

Make the money-spinner spin!
For you only stand to win,
And you'll never with dishonesty be twitted.

For nobody can know,
To a million or so,
To what extent your capital's committed!

CHORUS
No, nobody can know, etc.

If you come to grief, and creditors are craving
(For nothing that is planned by mortal head
Is certain in this Vale of Sorrow—saving
That one's Liability is Limited),—
Do you suppose that signifies perdition?
If so, you're but a monetary dunce—
You merely file a Winding-Up Petition,
And start another Company at once!
Though a Rothschild you may be
In your own capacity,
As a Company you've come to utter sorrow—
But the Liquidators say,
"Never mind—you needn't pay,"
So you start another company to-morrow!

CHORUS
But the liquidators say, etc.

KING
Well, at first sight it strikes us as dishonest,
But if its's good enough for virtuous England—
The first commercial country in the world—
It's good enough for us.

SCAPHIO, PHANTIS, TARARA (aside to the KING)
You'd best take care—
Please recollect we have not been consulted.

KING
And do I understand that Great Britain
Upon this Joint Stock principle is governed?

MR GOLDBURY
We haven't come to that, exactly—but
We're tending rapidly in that direction.
The date's not distant.

KING (enthusiastically)
We will be before you!
We'll go down in posterity renowned
As the First Sovereign in Christendom

Who registered his Crown and Country under
The Joint Stock Company's Act of Sixty-Two.

ALL
Ulahlica!

SOLO—**KING**
Henceforward, of a verity,
With Fame ourselves we link—
We'll go down to Posterity
Of sovereigns all the pink!

SCAPHIO, PHANTIS and TARARA (aside to KING)
If you've the mad temerity
Our wishes thus to blink,
You'll go down to Posterity,
Much earlier than you think!

TARARA (correcting them)
He'll go up to Posterity,
If I inflict the blow!

SCAPHIO and PHANTIS (angrily)
He'll go down to Posterity—
We think we ought to know!

TARARA (explaining)
He'll go up to Posterity,
Blown up with dynamite!

SCAPHIO and PHANTIS (apologetically)
He'll go up to Posterity,
Of course he will, you're right!

ENSEMBLE

KING, LADY SOPHY, NEKAYA, KALYBA, CALYNX and CHORUS	**SCAPHIO, PHANTIS, and TARARA** (aside)	**FITZBATTLEAXE and ZARA** (aside)
Henceforward of a verity,	If he has the temerity	Who love with all sincerity;
With fame ourselves we link	Our wishes thus to blink	Their lives may safely link.
And go down to Posterity,	He'll go up to Posterity	And as for our posterity
Of sovereigns all pink!	Much earlier than they think!	We don't care what they think!

CHORUS
Let's seal this mercantile pact—
The step we ne'er shall rue—
It gives whatever we lacked—
The statement's strictly true.

All hail, astonishing Fact!
All hail, Invention new—
The Joint Stock Company's Act—
The Act of Sixty-Two!

END OF ACT I

Scene — Throne Room in the Palace. Night.

FITZBATTLEAXE discovered, singing to ZARA.

RECITATIVE—**FITZBATTLEAXE**
Oh, Zara, my beloved one, bear with me!
Ah, do not laugh at my attempted C!
Repent not, mocking maid, thy girlhood's choice—
The fervour of my love affects my voice!

SONG—**FITZBATTLEAXE**
A tenor, all singers above
(This doesn't admit of a question),
Should keep himself quiet,
Attend to his diet
And carefully nurse his digestion;
But when he is madly in love
It's certain to tell on his singing—
You can't do the proper chromatics
With proper emphatics
When anguish your bosom is wringing!
When distracted with worries in plenty,
And his pulse is a hundred and twenty,
And his fluttering bosom the slave of mistrust is,
A tenor can't do himself justice,
Now observe—(sings a high note),
You see, I can't do myself justice!
I could sing if my fervour were mock,
It's easy enough if you're acting—
But when one's emotion
Is born of devotion
You mustn't be over-exacting.
One ought to be firm as a rock
To venture a shake in vibrato,
When fervour's expected
Keep cool and collected

Or never attempt agitato.
But, of course, when his tongue is of leather,
And his lips appear pasted together,
And his sensitive palate as dry as a crust is,
A tenor can't do himself justice.
Now observe—(sings a high note),
It's no use—I can't do myself justice!

ZARA

Why, Arthur, what does it matter? When the higher
Qualities of the heart are all that can be desired, the higher
notes of the voice are matters of comparative insignificance.
Who thinks slightingly of the cocoanut because it is husky?
Besides (demurely), you are not singing for an engagement
(putting her hand in his), you have that already!

FITZBATTLEAXE

How good and wise you are! How unerringly your practiced
brain winnows the wheat from the chaff—the material from
the merely incidental!

ZARA

My Girton training, Arthur. At Girton all is wheat, and idle chaff is never heard within its walls! But tell
me, is not all working marvelously well? Have not our Flowers of Progress more than justified their
name?

FITZBATTLEAXE

We have indeed done our best. Captain Corcoran and I have, in concert, thoroughly remodeled the
sister-services—and upon so sound a basis that the South Pacific trembles at the name of Utopia!

ZARA

How clever of you!

FITZBATTLEAXE

Clever? Not a bit. It's easy as possible when the Admiralty and Horse Guards are not there to interfere.
And so with the others. Freed from the trammels imposed upon them by idle Acts of Parliament, all
have given their natural talents full play and introduced reforms which, even in England, were never
dreamt of!

ZARA

But perhaps the most beneficent changes of all has been effected by Mr. Goldbury, who, discarding the
exploded theory that some strange magic lies hidden in the number Seven, has applied the Limited
Liability principle to individuals, and every man, woman, and child is now a Company Limited with
liability restricted to the amount of his declared Capital! There is not a christened baby in Utopia who
has not Already issued his little Prospectus!

FITZBATTLEAXE

Marvelous is the power of a Civilization which can transmute, by a word, a Limited Income into an Income Limited.

ZARA
Reform has not stopped here—it has been applied even to the costume of our people. Discarding their own barbaric dress, the natives of our land have unanimously adopted the tasteful fashions of England in all their rich entirety. Scaphio and Phantis have undertaken a contract to supply the whole of Utopia with clothing designed upon the most approved English models—and the first Drawing-Room under the new state of things is to be held here this evening.

FITZBATTLEAXE
But Drawing-Rooms are always held in the afternoon.

ZARA
Ah, we've improved upon that. We all look so much better by candlelight! And when I tell you, dearest, that my Court train has just arrived, you will understand that I am longing to go and try it on.

FITZBATTLEAXE
Then we must part?

ZARA
Necessarily, for a time.

FITZBATTLEAXE
Just as I wanted to tell you, with all the passionate enthusiasm of my nature, how deeply, how devotedly I love you!

ZARA
Hush! Are these the accents of a heart that really feels? True love does not indulge in declamation—its voice is sweet, and soft, and low. The west wind whispers when he woos the poplars!

DUET—**ZARA and FITZBATTLEAXE**

ZARA
Words of love too loudly spoken
Ring their own untimely knell;
Noisy vows are rudely broken,
Soft the song of Philomel.
Whisper sweetly, whisper slowly,
Hour by hour and day by day;
Sweet and low as accents holy
Are the notes of lover's lay.

BOTH
Sweet and low, etc.

FITZBATTLEAXE
Let the conqueror, flushed with glory,

Bid his noisy clarions bray;
Lovers tell their artless story
In a whispered virelay.
False is he whose vows alluring
Make the listening echoes ring;
Sweet and low when all-enduring
Are the songs that lovers sing!

BOTH
Sweet and low, etc.

(Exit ZARA. Enter KING dressed as Field-Marshal.)

KING
To a Monarch who has been accustomed to the uncontrolled use of his limbs, the costume of a British Field-Marshal is, perhaps, at first, a little cramping. Are you sure that this is all right? It's not a practical joke, is it? No one has a keener sense of humor than I have, but the First Statutory Cabinet Council of Utopia Limited must be conducted with dignity and impressiveness. Now, where are the other five who signed the Articles of Association?

FITZBATTLEAXE
Sir, they are here.

(Enter LORD DRAMALEIGH, CAPTAIN CORCORAN, SIR BAILEY BARRE, Mr BLUSHINGTON, and MR GOLDBURY from different entrances.)

KING
Oh! (Addressing them) Gentlemen, our daughter holds her first Drawing-Room in half an hour, and we shall have time to make our half-yearly report in the interval. I am necessarily unfamiliar with the forms of an English Cabinet Council—perhaps the Lord Chamberlain will kindly put us In the way of doing the thing properly, and with due regard to the solemnity of the occasion.

LORD DRAMALEIGH
Certainly—nothing simpler. Kindly bring your chairs forward—His Majesty will, of course, preside.

(They range their chairs across stage like Christy Minstrels. KING sits center, LORD DRAMALEIGH on his left, MR GOLDBURY on his right, CAPTAIN CORCORAN left of LORD DRAMALEIGH, CAPTAIN FITZBATTLEAXE right of MR GOLDBURY, MR BLUSHINGTON extreme right, SIR BAILEY BARRE extreme left.)

KING
Like this?

LORD DRAMALEIGH
Like this.

KING

We take your word for it that this is all right. You are not making fun of us? This is in accordance with the practice at the Court of St. James's?

LORD DRAMALEIGH
Well, it is in accordance with the practice at the Court Of St. James's Hall.

KING
Oh! it seems odd, but never mind.

SONG—**KING**
Society has quite forsaken all her wicked courses.
Which empties our police courts, and abolishes divorces.

CHORUS
Divorce is nearly obsolete in England.

KING
No tolerance we show to undeserving rank and splendour;
For the higher his position is, the greater the offender.

CHORUS
That's maxim that is prevalent in England.

KING
No peeress at our drawing-room before the Presence passes
Who wouldn't be accepted by the lower middle-classes.
Each shady dame, whatever be her rank, is bowed out
neatly.

CHORUS
In short, this happy country has been Anglicized completely
Is really is surprising
What a thorough Anglicizing
We have brought about—Utopia's quite another land;
In her enterprising movements,
She is England—with improvements,
Which we dutifully offer to our motherland!

KING
Our city we have beautified—we've done it willy-nilly—
And all that isn't Belgrave Square is Strand and
Piccadilly.

CHORUS
We haven't any slummeries in England!

KING
The chamberlain our native stage has purged beyond a question.

Of "risky" situation and indelicate suggestion;
No piece is tolerated if it's costumed indiscreetly—

CHORUS
In short this happy country has been Anglicized completely!
It really is surprising, etc.

KING
Our peerage we've remodelled on an intellectual basis,
Which certainly is rough on our hereditary races—

CHORUS
We are going to remodel it in England.

KING
The Brewers and the Cotton Lords no longer seek admission,
And literary merit meets with proper recognition—

CHORUS
As literary merit does in England!

KING
Who knows but we may count among our intellectual Chickens
Like you, an Earl of Thackery and p'r'aps a Duke of Dickens—
Lord Fildes and Viscount Millais (when they come) we'll welcome sweetly—

CHORUS
In short, this happy country has been Anglicized completely! It really is surprising, etc.

(At the end all rise and replace their chairs.)

KING
Now, then for our first Drawing-Room. Where are the
Princesses? What an extraordinary thing it is that since
European looking-glasses have been supplied to the
Royal bedrooms my daughters are invariably late!

LORD DRAMALEIGH
Sir, their Royal Highnesses await your pleasure in the Ante-room.

KING
Oh. Then request them to do us the favor to enter at once.

(Enter all the Royal Household, including (besides the LORD CHAMBERLAIN) the Vice-Chamberlain, the
Master of the Horse, the Master of the Buckhounds, the Lord High Treasurer, the Lord Steward, the
Comptroller of the Household, the Lord-in-Waiting, the Field Officer in Brigade Waiting, the Gold and
Silver Stick, and the Gentlemen Ushers. Then enter the three Princesses (their Trains carried by Pages of
Honor), LADY SOPHY, and the Ladies-in-Waiting.)

KING
My daughters, we are about to attempt a very solemn ceremonial, so no giggling, if you please. Now, my Lord Chamber-lain, we are ready.

LORD DRAMALEIGH
Then, ladies and gentlemen, places, if you please. His Majesty will take his place in front of the throne, and will be so obliging as to embrace all the debutantes.

(LADY SOPHY much shocked.)

KING
What—must I really?

LORD DRAMALEIGH
Absolutely indispensable.

KING
More jam for the Palace Peeper!

(The KING takes his place in front of the throne, the PRINCESS ZARA on his left, the two younger PRINCESSES on the left of ZARA.)

KING
Now, is every one in his place?

LORD DRAMALEIGH
Every one is in his place.

KING
Then let the revels commence.

(Enter the LADIES attending the Drawing-Room. They give their cards to the Groom-in-Waiting, who passes them to the Lord-in-Waiting, who passes them to the Vice-Chamberlain, who passes them to the Lord Chamberlain, who reads the names to the KING as each LADY approaches. The LADIES curtsey in succession to the KING and the three PRINCESSES, and pass out. When all the presentations have been accomplished, the KING, PRINCESSES, and LADY SOPHY come forward, and all the LADIES re-enter.)

RECITATIVE—**KING**
This ceremonial our wish displays
To copy all Great Britain's courtly ways.
Though lofty aims catastrophe entail,
We'll gloriously succeed or nobly fail!

UNACCOMPANIED CHORUS
Eagle High in Cloudland soaring—
Sparrow twittering on a reed—
Tiger in the jungle roaring—

Frightened fawn in grassy mead—
Let the eagle, not the sparrow,
Be the object of your arrow—
Fix the tiger with your eye—
Pass the fawn in pity by.
Glory then will crown the day—
Glory, glory, anyway!

Exit all.

Enter SCAPHIO and PHANTIS, now dressed as judges in red and ermine Robes and undress wigs. They come down stage melodramatically—working together.

DUET—**SCAPHIO and PHANTIS**

SCAPHIO
With fury deep we burn

PHANTIS
We do—

SCAPHIO
We fume with smothered rage—

PHANTIS
We do—

SCAPHIO
These Englishmen who rule supreme,
Their undertaking they redeem
By stifling every harmless scheme
In which we both engage—

PHANTIS
They do—

SCAPHIO
 In which we both engage—

PHANTIS
We think it is our turn—

SCAPHIO
We do—

PHANTIS
We think our turn has come—

SCAPHIO
We do.

PHANTIS
These Englishmen, they must prepare
To seek at once their native air.
The King as heretofore, we swear,
Shall be beneath our thumb—

SCAPHIO
He shall—

PHANTIS
Shall be beneath out thumb—

SCAPHIO
He shall.

BOTH (with great energy)
For this mustn't be, and this won't do.
If you'll back me, then I'll back you,
No, this won't do,
No, this mustn't be.
With fury deep we burn...

Enter the KING.

KING
Gentlemen, gentlemen—really! This unseemly display of energy within the Royal precincts is altogether unpardonable. Pray, what do you complain of?

SCAPHIO (furiously)
What do we complain of? Why, through the innovations introduced by the Flowers of Progress all our harmless schemes for making a provision for our old age are ruined. Our Matrimonial Agency is at a standstill, our Cheap Sherry business is in bankruptcy, our Army Clothing contracts are paralyzed, and even our Society paper, the Palace Peeper, is practically defunct!

KING
Defunct? Is that so? Dear, dear, I am truly sorry.

SCAPHIO
Are you aware that Sir Bailey Barre has introduced a law of libel by which all editors of scurrilous newspapers are publicly flogged—as in England? And six of our editors have resigned in succession! Now, the editor of a scurrilous paper can stand a good deal—he takes a private thrashing as a matter of course—it's considered in his salary—but no gentleman likes to be publicly flogged.

KING
Naturally. I shouldn't like it myself.

PHANTIS
Then our Burlesque Theater is absolutely ruined!

KING
Dear me. Well, theatrical property is not what it was.

PHANTIS
Are you aware that the Lord Chamberlain, who has his own views as to the best means of elevating the national drama, has declined to license any play that is not in blank Verse and three hundred years old—as in England?

SCAPHIO
And as if that wasn't enough, the County Councillor has ordered a four-foot wall to be built up right across the proscenium, in case of fire—as in England.

PHANTIS
It's so hard on the company—who are liable to be roasted alive—and this has to be met by enormously increased salaries—as in England.

SCAPHIO
You probably know that we've contracted to supply the entire nation with a complete English outfit. But perhaps you do not know that, when we send in our bills, our customers plead liability limited to a declared capital of eighteen pence, and apply to be dealt with under the Winding-up Act—as in England?

KING
Really, gentlemen, this is very irregular. If you will
Be so good as to formulate a detailed list of your
Grievances in writing, addressed to the Secretary of Utopia Limited,
They will be laid before the Board, in due course, at their next monthly meeting.

SCAPHIO
Are we to understand that we are defied?

KING
That is the idea I intended to convey.

PHANTIS
Defied! We are defied!

SCAPHIO (furiously)
Take care—you know our powers. Trifle with us, and you die!

TRIO—**SCAPHIO, PHANTIS and KING**

SCAPHIO
If you think that, when banded in unity,

We may both be defied with impunity,
You are sadly misled of a verity!

PHANTIS
If you value repose and tranquility,
You'll revert to a state of docility,
Or prepare to regret your temerity!

KING
If my speech is unduly refractory
You will find it a course satisfactory
At an early Board meeting to show it up.
Though if proper excuse you can trump any,
You may wind up a Limited Company,
You cannot conveniently blow it up!

(SCAPHIO and PHANTISs thoroughly baffled)

KING (Dancing quietly)
Whene'er I chance to baffle you
I, also, dance a step or two—
Of this now guess the hidden sense:

(SCAPHIO and PHANTIS consider the question as KING continues Dancing quietly—then give it up.)

It means complete indifference!

SCAPHIO and PHANTIS
Of course it does—indifference!
It means complete indifference!

(KING dancing quietly. SCAPHIO and PHANTIS dancing furiously.)

SCAPHIO and PHANTIS
As we've a dance for every mood
With pas de trois we will conclude,
What this may mean you all may guess—
It typifies remorselessness!

KING
It means unruffled cheerfulness!

(KING dances off placidly as SCAPHIO and PHANTISs dance furiously.)

PHANTIS (breathless)
He's right—we are helpless! He's no longer a human being—he's a Corporation, and so long as he confines himself to his Articles of Association we can't touch him! What are we to do?

SCAPHIO
Do? Raise a Revolution, repeal the Act of Sixty-Two, reconvert him into an individual, and insist on his immediate explosion! (TARARA enters) Tarara, come here; you're the very man we want.

TARARA
Certainly, allow me.

(Offers a cracker to each; they snatch them away impatiently.)

That's rude.

SCAPHIO
We have no time for idle forms. You wish to succeed to
The throne?

TARARA
Naturally.

SCAPHIO
Then you won't unless you join us. The King has defied us, and, as matters stand, we are helpless. So are you. We must devise some plot at once to bring the people about his ears.

TARARA
A plot?

PHANTIS
Yes, a plot of superhuman subtlety. Have you such a
Thing about you?

TARARA (feeling)
No, I think not. No. There's one on my dressing-table.

SCAPHIO
We can't wait—we must concoct one at once, and put it
Into execution without delay. There is not a moment to spare!

TRIO—SCAPHIO, PHANTIS and TARARA

ENSEMBLE
With wily brain upon the spot
A private plot we'll plan,
The most ingenious private plot
Since private plots began.
That's understood. So far we've got
And, striking while the iron's hot,
We'll now determine like a shot
The details of this private plot.

SCAPHIO
I think we ought—(whispers)

PHANTIS and TARARA
Such bosh I never heard!

PHANTIS
Ah! happy thought!—(whispers)

SCAPHIO and TARARA
How utterly dashed absurd!

TARARA
I'll tell you how—(whispers)

SCAPHIO and PHANTIS
Why, what put that in your head?

SCAPHIO
I've got it now—(whispers)

PHANTIS and TARARA
Oh, take him away to bed!

PHANTIS
Oh, put him to bed!

TARARA
Oh, put him to bed!

SCAPHIO
What, put me to bed?

PHANTIS and TARARA
Yes, certainly put him to bed!

SCAPHIO
But, bless me, don't you see—

PHANTIS
Do listen to me, I pray—

TARARA
It certainly seems to me—

SCAPHIO
Bah—this is the only way!

PHANTIS
It's rubbish absurd you growl!

TARARA
You talk ridiculous stuff!

SCAPHIO
You're a drivelling barndoor owl!

PHANTIS
You're a vapid and vain old muff!

(ALL, coming down to audience.)
So far we haven't quite solved the plot—
They're not a very ingenious lot—
But don't be unhappy,
It's still on the tapis,
We'll presently hit on a capital plot!

SCAPHIO
Suppose we all—(whispers)

PHANTIS
Now there I think you're right.
Then we might all—(whispers)

TARARA
That's true, we certainly might.
I'll tell you what—(whispers)

SCAPHIO
We will if we possibly can.
Then on the spot—(whispers)

PHANTIS and TARARA
Bravo! A capital plan!

SCAPHIO
That's exceedingly neat and new!

PHANTIS
Exceedingly new and neat.

TARARA
I fancy that that will do.

SCAPHIO
It's certainly very complete.

PHANTIS
Well done you sly old sap!

TARARA
Bravo, you cunning old mole!

SCAPHIO
You very ingenious chap!

PHANTIS
You intellectual soul!

(ALL, coming down and addressing audience.)

At last a capital plan we've got
We won't say how and we won't say what:
It's safe in my noddle—
Now off we will toddle,
And slyly develop this capital plot!

(Business. Exeunt SCAPHIO and PHANTIS in one direction and TARARA in the other.)

(Enter LORD DRAMALEIGH and MR GOLDBURY)

LORD DRAMALEIGH
Well, what do you think of our first South Pacific
Drawing-Room? Allowing for a slight difficulty with the
trains, and a little want of familiarity with the use of
the rouge-pot, it was, on the whole, a meritorious affair?

MR GOLDBURY
My dear Dramaleigh, it redounds infinitely to your credit.

LORD DRAMALEIGH
One or two judicious innovations, I think?

MR GOLDBURY
Admirable. The cup of tea and the plate of mixed
Biscuits were a cheap and effective inspiration.

LORD DRAMALEIGH
Yes—my idea entirely. Never been done before.

MR GOLDBURY
Pretty little maids, the King's youngest daughters, but timid.

LORD DRAMALEIGH

That'll wear off. Young.

MR. GOLDBURY
That'll wear off. Ha! here they come, by George! And with-out the Dragon! What can they have done with her?

(Enter NEKAYA and KALYBA timidly.)

NEKAYA
Oh, if you please, Lady Sophy has sent us in here,
Because Zara and Captain Fitzbattleaxe are going on, in the
garden, in a manner which no well-conducted young ladies ought to witness.

LORD DRAMALEIGH
Indeed, we are very much obliged to her Ladyship.

KALYBA
Are you? I wonder why.

NEKAYA
 Don't tell us if it's rude.

LORD DRAMALEIGH
Rude? Not at all. We are obliged to Lady Sophy because
She has afforded us the pleasure of seeing you.

NEKAYA
I don't think you ought to talk to us like that.

KALYBA
It's calculated to turn our heads.

NEKAYA
Attractive girls cannot be too particular.

KALYBA
Oh pray, pray do not take advantage of our unprotected innocence.

MR. GOLDBURY
Pray be reassured—you are in no danger whatever.

LORD DRAMALEIGH
But may I ask—is this extreme delicacy—this shrinking sensitiveness—a general characteristic of Utopian young ladies?

NEKAYA
Oh no; we are crack specimens.

KALYBA

We are the pick of the basket. Would you mind not coming quite so near? Thank you.

NEKAYA

And please don't look at us like that; it unsettles us.

KALYBA

And we don't like it. At least, we do like it; but it's wrong.

NEKAYA

We have enjoyed the inestimable privilege of being educated by a most refined and easily shocked English lady, on the very strictest English principles.

MR GOLDBURY

But, my dear young ladies—-

KALYBA

Oh, don't! You mustn't. It's too affectionate.

NEKAYA

It really does unsettle us.

MR GOLDBURY

Are you really under the impression that English girls
Are so ridiculously demure? Why, an English girl of the
Highest type is the best, the most beautiful, the bravest, and
The brightest creature that Heaven has conferred upon this
World of ours. She is frank, open-hearted, and fearless, and
Never shows in so favorable a light as when she gives her
Own blameless impulses full play!

NEKAYA and KALYBA

Oh, you shocking story!

MR GOLDBURY

Not at all. I'm speaking the strict truth. I'll tell
You all about her.

SONG—**MR GOLDBURY**
A wonderful joy our eyes to bless,
In her magnificent comeliness,
Is an English girl of eleven stone two,
And five foot ten in her dancing shoe!
She follows the hounds, and on the pounds—
The "field" tails off and the muffs diminish—

Over the hedges and brooks she bounds,
Straight as a crow, from find to finish.

At cricket, her kin will lose or win—
She and her maids, on grass and clover,
Eleven maids out—eleven maids in—
And perhaps an occasional "maiden over!"

Go search the world and search the sea,
Then come you home and sing with me
There's no such gold and no such pearl
As a bright and beautiful English girl!

With a ten-mile spin she stretches her limbs,
She golfs, she punts, she rows, she swims—
She plays, she sings, she dances, too,
From ten or eleven til all is blue!
At ball or drum, til small hours come
(Chaperon's fans concealing her yawning)
She'll waltz away like a teetotum.
And never go home til daylight's dawning.
Lawn-tennis may share her favours fair—
Her eyes a-dance, and her cheeks a-glowing—
Down comes her hair, but then what does she care?
It's all her own and it's worth the showing!
Go search the world, etc.

Her soul is sweet as the ocean air,
For prudery knows no haven there;
To find mock-modesty, please apply
To the conscious blush and the downcast eye.
Rich in the things contentment brings,
In every pure enjoyment wealthy,
Blithe and beautiful bird she sings,
For body and mind are hale and healthy.
Her eyes they thrill with right goodwill—
Her heart is light as a floating feather—
As pure and bright as the mountain rill
That leaps and laughs in the Highland heather!
Go search the world, etc.

QUARTET

NEKAYA
Then I may sing and play?

LORD DRAMALEIGH
You may!

KALYBA
Then I may laugh and shout?

MR GOLDBURY
No doubt!

NEKAYA
These maxims you endorse?

LORD DRAMALEIGH
Of course!

KALYBA
You won't exclaim "Oh fie!"

MR. GOLDBURY
Not I!

MR GOLDBURY
Whatever you are—be that:
Whatever you say—be true:
Straightforwardly act—
Be honest—in fact,
Be nobody else but you.

LORD DRAMALEIGH
Give every answer pat—
Your character true unfurl;
And when it is ripe,
You'll then be a type
Of a capital English girl.

ALL
Oh sweet surprise—oh, dear delight,
To find it undisputed quite,
All musty, fusty rules despite
That Art is wrong and Nature right!

NEKAYA
When happy I,
With laughter glad
I'll wake the echoes fairly,
And only sigh
When I am sad—
And that will be but rarely!

KALYBA
I'll row and fish,
And gallop, soon—
No longer be a prim one—

And when I wish
To hum a tune,
It needn't be a hymn one?

GOLDBURY and LORD DRAMALEIGH
No, no!
It needn't be a hymn one!

ALL (dancing)
Oh, sweet surprise and dear delight
To find it undisputed quite—
All musty, fusty rules despite—
That Art is wrong and Nature right!

(Dance, and off)

(Enter LADY SOPHY)

RECITATIVE—**LADY SOPHY**
Oh, would some demon power the gift impart
To quell my over-conscientious heart—
Unspeak the oaths that never had been spoken,
And break the vows that never should be broken!

SONG—**LADY SOPHY**
When but a maid of fifteen year,
Unsought—unplighted—
Short petticoated—and, I fear,
Still shorter-sighted—
I made a vow, one early spring,
That only to some spotless King
Who proof of blameless life could bring
I'd be united.
For I had read, not long before,
Of blameless kings in fairy lore,
And thought the race still flourished here—
Well, well—
I was a maid of fifteen year!

(The KING enters and overhears this verse)

Each morning I pursued my game
(An early riser);
For spotless monarchs I became
An advertiser:
But all in vain I searched each land,
So, kingless, to my native strand
Returned, a little older, and

A good deal wiser!

I learnt that spotless King and Prince
Have disappeared some ages since—
Even Paramount's angelic grace—
Ah me!—
Is but a mask on Nature's face!

(KING comes forward)

KING
Ah, Lady Sophy—then you love me!
For so you sing—

LADY SOPHY
(Indignant and surprise. Producing "Palace Peeper")
No, by the stars that shine above me,
Degraded King!
For while these rumours, through the city bruited,
Remain uncontradicted, unrefuted,
The object thou of my aversion rooted,
Repulsive thing!

KING
Be just—the time is now at hand
When truth may published be.
These paragraphs were written and
Contributed by me!

LADY SOPHY
By you? No, no!

KING
Yes, yes. I swear, by me!
I, caught in Scaphio's ruthless toil,
Contributed the lot!

LADY SOPHY
That that is why you did not boil
The author on the spot!

KING
And that is why I did not boil
The author on the spot!

LADY SOPHY
I couldn't think why you did not boil!

KING
But I know why I did not boil
The author on the spot!

DUET—**LADY SOPHY and KING**

LADY SOPHY
Oh, the rapture unrestrained
Of a candid retractation!
For my sovereign has deigned
A convincing explanation—
And the clouds that gathered o'er
All have vanished in the distance,
And the Kings of fairy lore
One, at least, is in existence!

KING
Oh, the skies are blue above,
And the earth is red and rosal,
Now the lady of my love
Has accepted my proposal!
For that asinorum pons
I have crossed without assistance,
And of prudish paragons
One, at least, is in existence!

(KING and LADY SOPHY dance gracefully. While this is going on LORD DRAMALEIGH enters unobserved with NEKAYA and CAPTAIN FITZBATTLEAXE. The two girls direct ZARA'S attention to the KING and LADY SOPHY, Who are still dancing affectionately together. At this point the KING kisses LADY SOPHY, which causes the PRINCESSES to make an exclamation. The KING and LADY SOPHY are at first much confused at being detected, but eventually throw off all reserve, and the four couples break into a wild Tarantella, and at the end exeunt severally.)

Enter all the MALE CHORUS, in great excitement, for various entrances, led by SCAPHIO, PHANTIS, and TARARA, and followed by the FEMALE CHORUS.

CHORUS
Upon our sea-girt land
At our enforced command
Reform has laid her hand
Like some remorseless ogress—
And made us darkly rue
The deeds she dared to do—
And all is owing to
Those hated Flowers of Progress!

So down with them!
So down with them!

Reform's a hated ogress.
So down with them!
So down with them!
Down with the Flowers of Progress!

(Flourish. Enter KING, his THREE DAUGHTERS, LADY SOPHY, and the FLOWERS OF PROGRESS)

KING
What means this most unmannerly irruption?
Is this your gratitude for boons conferred?

SCAPHIO
Boons? Bah! A fico for such boons, say we!
These boons have brought Utopia to a standstill!
Our pride and boast—the Army and the Navy—
Have both been reconstructed and remodeled
Upon so irresistible a basis
That all the neighboring nations have disarmed—
And War's impossible! Your County Councillor
Has passed such drastic Sanitary laws
That all doctors dwindle, starve, and die!
The laws, remodeled by Sir Bailey Barre,
Have quite extinguished crime and litigation:
The lawyers starve, and all the jails are let
As model lodgings for the working-classes!
In short—Utopia, swamped by dull Prosperity,
Demands that these detested Flowers of Progress
Be sent about their business, and affairs
Restored to their original complexion!

KING (to ZARA)
My daughter, this is a very unpleasant state
Of things. What is to be done?

ZARA
I don't know—I don't understand it. We must have omitted something.

KING
Omitted something? Yes, that's all very well, but—

(SIR BAILEY BARRE whispers to ZARA.)

ZARA (suddenly)
Of course! Now I remember! Why, I had forgotten the most essential element of all!

KING
And that is?—

ZARA

Government by Party! Introduce that great and glorious element—at once the bulwark and foundation of England's greatness—and all will be well! No political measures will endure, because one Party will assuredly undo all that the other Party has done; and while grouse is to be shot, and foxes worried to death, the legislative action of the county-try will be at a standstill. Then there will be sickness in plenty, endless lawsuits, crowded jails, interminable confusion in the Army and Navy, and, in short, general and unexampled prosperity!

ALL

Ulahlica! Ulahlica!

PHANTIS (aside)

Baffled!

SCAPHIO

But an hour will come!

KING

Your hour has come already—away with them, and let them wait my will!

(SCAPHIO and PHANTIS are led off in custody.)

From this moment Government by Party is adopted, with all its attendant blessings; and henceforward Utopia will no longer be a Monarchy Limited, but, what is a great deal better, a Limited Monarchy!

FINALE

ZARA

There's a little group of isles beyond the wave—
So tiny, you might almost wonder where it is—
That nation is the bravest of the brave,
And cowards are the rarest of all rarities.
The proudest nations kneel at her command;
She terrifies all foreign-born rapscallions;
And holds the peace of Europe in her hand
With half a score invincible battalions!

Such, at least, is the tale
Which is born on the gale,
From the island which dwells in the sea.
Let us hope, for her sake
That she makes no mistake—
That she's all the professes to be!

KING

Oh, may we copy all her maxims wise,
And imitate her virtues and her charities;
And may we, by degrees, acclimatize

Her Parliamentary peculiarities!
By doing so, we shall in course of time,
Regenerate completely our entire land—
Great Britain is the monarchy sublime,
To which some add (others do not) Ireland.
Such at least is the tale, etc.

CURTAIN.

W.S. Gilbert – A Short Biography

Sir William Schwenck Gilbert was born on November 18th, 1836 at 17 Southampton Street, Strand, London. His father, also named William, was a naval surgeon, who later became a writer of novels and short stories, some of which were illustrated by his son. Gilbert's mother was the former Anne Mary Bye Morris (1812–1888), the daughter of Thomas Morris, an apothecary.

Gilbert's parents were distant and stern, and there was no close bond between either themselves or their children (the marriage was to eventually break up in 1876). Gilbert had three younger sisters, Jane Morris, Anne Maude Mary Florence.

As a child, Gilbert was nicknamed "Bab".

The family travelled to Italy in 1838 and then France before finally returning to settle in London in 1847.

Gilbert was educated in Boulogne, France from age seven, then at Western Grammar School, Brompton, London, before the Great Ealing School, where he became head boy and wrote plays for school performances. He then attended King's College London, graduating in 1856.

His first thought for a career was to take examinations for a commission in the Royal Artillery, but the Crimean War had just ended and with fewer recruits needed only a commission in a line regiment was available. He opted instead for the Civil Service and was an assistant clerk in the Privy Council Office for four years. He hated it. In 1859 he joined the Militia, a part-time volunteer force, and served until 1878, as his other work allowed, and reached the rank of Captain.

To supplement his income Gilbert wrote a variety of stories, comic rants, theatre reviews (many in the form of a parody of the play being reviewed), and, using the pseudonym of his childhood nickname, "Bab" illustrated poems for several comic magazines, primarily Fun, started in 1861. His work was also published in the Cornhill Magazine, London Society, Tinsley's Magazine and Temple Bar. Gilbert was also the London correspondent for L'Invalide Russe and a drama critic for the Illustrated London Times. In the 1860s he also contributed to Tom Hood's Christmas annuals, to Saturday Night, the Comic News and the Savage Club Papers.

The poems, illustrated humorously by Gilbert, proved immensely popular and were reprinted in book form as the Bab Ballads. He would later return to many of these as source material for his plays and comic operas.

In 1863 he received a bequest of £300 allowing him to leave the civil service and attempt a career as a barrister. Unfortunately, he managed to attract few clients.

However, these events happily coincided with his first professionally produced play; Uncle Baby, which ran for seven weeks in the autumn of 1863.

In 1865–66, Gilbert collaborated with Charles Millward on several pantomimes, including Hush-a-Bye, Baby, On the Tree Top, or, Harlequin Fortunia, King Frog of Frog Island, and the Magic Toys of Lowther Arcade (1866).

Gilbert's first solo success, however, came a few days after Hush-a-Bye Baby premiered. His friend and mentor, Tom Robertson, was asked to deliver a pantomime within two weeks. Robertson couldn't and recommended Gilbert who took the job. Written and rushed to the stage in 10 days, Dulcamara, or the Little Duck and the Great Quack, a burlesque of Gaetano Donizetti's L'elisir d'amore, proved very popular. This led to a long series of further Gilbert opera burlesques, pantomimes and farces, full of dreadful puns, but showing signs of the satire that would later be such an integral part of Gilbert's work.

After a failed relationship with the novelist Annie Thomas, Gilbert married Lucy Agnes Turner, whom he affectionately called "Kitty", in 1867; she was 11 years his junior. They were socially active both in London and later at their new home at Grim's Dyke, often holding dinner parties. Although they had no children they had many pets, including several exotic ones.

Next followed Gilbert's biggest success so far; his penultimate operatic parody, Robert the Devil, a burlesque of Giacomo Meyerbeer's opera, Robert le diable, part of a triple bill that opened the Gaiety Theatre, London in 1868. It ran for over 100 nights.

In Victorian theatre, Gilbert's burlesques were considered very tasteful compared to the offerings of others. He would now move away from burlesque to plays with original plots and fewer puns. His first was An Old Score in 1869.

Theatre, at this time had fallen into disrepute. London was awash with poorly translated French operettas and cheaply written, prurient Victorian burlesques. From 1869 to 1875, Gilbert joined with Thomas German Reed (and his wife Priscilla), whose Gallery of Illustration sought to regain some of theatre's lost respect with family entertainments. This would be so successful that by 1885 Gilbert could safely state that original British plays were appropriate for an innocent 15-year-old girl to watch.

The initial work for the Gallery of Illustration, No Cards, was the first of six musical entertainments for the German Reeds, by Gilbert some with music composed by Thomas German Reed.

The German Reeds' intimate theatre allowed Gilbert to develop a personal style that would also cede to him control all aspects of production; set, costumes, direction and stage management.

Gilbert's first big hit at the Gallery of Illustration, Ages Ago, also opened in 1869. It marked the beginning of a collaboration with the composer Frederic Clay that would last seven years and cover four works. It was at a rehearsal for Ages Ago that Clay introduced Gilbert to Arthur Sullivan.

These musical works gave Gilbert a valuable education as a lyricist and he perfected the 'topsy-turvy' style that he had been developing in his Bab Ballads, where the humour was derived by setting up a ridiculous premise and following through on its logical consequences, however absurd they might be.

Ever busy he found time to create several 'fairy comedies' at the Haymarket Theatre. The premise was the idea of self-revelation by characters under the influence of magic or some supernatural experience. The first was The Palace of Truth (1870), based partly on a story by Madame de Genlis. In 1871, with Pygmalion and Galatea, one of seven plays that he produced that year, Gilbert scored his greatest hit to date. Together, these plays including The Wicked World (1873), Sweethearts (1874), and Broken Hearts (1875), did for Gilbert on the dramatic stage what the German Reed entertainments had done for him on the musical stage: they established that his talents were large and burgeoning, a writer of wide range, as comfortable with human drama as much as farcical humour.

Contemptorous with this period Gilbert pushed the satirical boundaries. He collaborated with Gilbert Arthur à Beckett on The Happy Land (1873), in part, a parody of his own The Wicked World, which was briefly banned because of its caricatures of Gladstone and his ministers. Similarly, The Realm of Joy (1873) was set in the lobby of a theatre performing a scandalous play (implied to be the Happy Land), with many jokes at the expense of the Lord Chamberlain (the "Lord High Disinfectant", as he's referred to in the play). In Charity (1874), however, Gilbert uses the freedom of the stage in a different way: to illuminate the contrasting ways in which society treated men and women who had sex outside of marriage. It was ground breaking and some see it as anticipating the 'problem plays' of Shaw and Ibsen.

Once established as a writer Gilbert was also the stage director, with strong, forceful opinions on how they should best be performed.

In Gilbert's 1874 burlesque, Rosencrantz and Guildenstern, the character Hamlet, in his speech to the players, sums up Gilbert's theory of comic acting: "I hold that there is no such antick fellow as your bombastical hero who doth so earnestly spout forth his folly as to make his hearers believe that he is unconscious of all incongruity". Again some say with this he prepared the ground for playwrights such as George Bernard Shaw and Oscar Wilde to be able to flourish.

Tom Robertson had "introduced Gilbert both to the revolutionary notion of disciplined rehearsals and to mise-en-scène or unity of style in the whole presentation – direction, design, music, acting." Like Robertson, Gilbert demanded discipline in his actors, that they know their lines, enunciate them clearly and keep to his stage directions, a new development for actors at the time. It also ushered in the replacement of the star with the disciplined ensemble.

Gilbert was meticulous in his preparations, making models of the stage and designing every action in advance. He refused to work with actors who challenged him. He was famous for demonstrating the action himself, even as he grew older. Such was his interest in standards that even during long runs and revivals, he closely supervised the performances of his plays, making sure that no one made additions or deletions.

Sir Arthur Seymour Sullivan, MVO was born on May 13th 1842 in Lambeth, London. His father, Thomas Sullivan, a military bandmaster, clarinetist and music teacher, was born in Ireland and raised in Chelsea, London, and his mother, Mary Clementina (née Coghlan, English born, of Irish and Italian descent. Thomas Sullivan was based from 1845 to 1857 at the Royal Military College, Sandhurst, where he was the bandmaster and taught music privately to supplement his income. Young Sullivan became proficient with many of the instruments in the band and had composed an anthem, "By the waters of Babylon", by the age of eight. While proudly observing his son's obvious musical talent, he knew, at first hand, how insecure a profession it was and discouraged him from pursuing it.

Three years later whilst at a private school in Bayswater, Sullivan persuaded his parents and headmaster to allow him to apply for membership in the choir of the Chapel Royal. There were concerns that Sullivan at nearly 12 years of age was too old to be a treble as his voice would soon break. But he was accepted and soon became a soloist and, by 1856, was promoted to "first boy". Troublingly, even at this age, Sullivan's health was delicate, and he was easily fatigued.

However, Sullivan flourished under the training of the Reverend Thomas Helmore, and began to compose anthems and songs. Helmore arranged for one pieces, "O Israel", to be published in 1855.

In 1856, the Royal Academy of Music awarded the first Mendelssohn Scholarship to the 14-year-old Sullivan, granting him a year's training at the academy. His principal teacher there was John Goss, whose own teacher had been a pupil of Mozart. Initially Sullivan studied piano.

Sullivan's scholarship was extended to a second year, and then a third so that he could study in Germany, at the Leipzig Conservatoire. There he was trained in Mendelssohn's ideas and techniques as well as being exposed to Schubert, Verdi, Bach, and Wagner. Sullivan was an eager pupil and always looking for inspiration. On a visit to a synagogue, he was so struck by some of the cadences and progressions in the music that three decades later he would recall them for use in his serious opera, Ivanhoe.

Though the scholarship in Leipzig, was for one year he stayed for three. Sullivan credited his Leipzig period with rapid and sustained musical growth. His graduation piece, in 1861, was a set of incidental music to Shakespeare's The Tempest. Revised and expanded, it was performed at the Crystal Palace in 1862, a year after his return to London. It was an immediate sensation. He began building a reputation as England's most promising young composer.

He now embarked on composing with a series of ambitious works, interspersed with hymns, parlour songs and other light pieces of a more commercial nature. These compositions could not support him financially, and from 1861 to 1872 he supplemented his income working as a church organist, a task he enjoyed, and as a music teacher, sometimes at the Crystal Palace School, which he hated and gave up as soon as his finances allowed. Sullivan also took an early chance to compose pieces for royalty with the wedding of the Prince of Wales in 1863.

Sullivan began to put voice and orchestra together with The Masque at Kenilworth (Birmingham Festival, 1864). For Covent Garden that same year he composed his first ballet, L'Île Enchantée.

1865 saw Sullivan initiated into Freemasonry and was Grand Organist of the United Grand Lodge of England in 1887 during Queen Victoria's Golden Jubilee.

In 1866, he premiered his Irish Symphony and Cello Concerto, his only works in these genres. In the same year, his Overture in C (In Memoriam), commemorating the recent death of his father, was a commission from the Norwich Festival.

His overture Marmion was premiered by the Philharmonic Society in 1867. The Times called it "another step in advance on the part of the only composer of any remarkable promise that just at present we can boast."

Sadly, his initial attempt at opera, The Sapphire Necklace (1863–64) with a libretto by Henry F. Chorley, was not produced and, apart from the Overture and two songs published separately, is now lost.

His first surviving opera, Cox and Box (1866), was written for a private performance. It then received charity performances in London and Manchester, and was later produced at the Gallery of Illustration, where it ran for an extraordinary 264 performances. His soon to be partner, W. S. Gilbert, writing in Fun magazine, announced the score as superior to F. C. Burnand's libretto.

In 1867 Sullivan and Burnand were commissioned by Thomas German Reed for a two-act opera, The Contrabandista (revised and expanded as The Chieftain in 1894), but it was a much more modest success.

Sullivan wrote a group of seven part songs in 1868, the best-known of which is "The Long Day Closes". His last major work of the 1860s was a short oratorio, The Prodigal Son, which premiered in Worcester Cathedral as part of the 1869 Three Choirs Festival to much praise.

The Overture di Ballo, Sullivan's most enduring work, was composed for the Birmingham Festival in 1870.

1871 was a busy year. Sullivan published his only song cycle, The Window; or, The Songs of the Wrens, to words by Tennyson, and wrote the first of a series of suites of incidental music for West End productions of Shakespeare plays. Later in the year he composed a dramatic cantata, On Shore and Sea, for the opening of the London International Exhibition, and the beautiful hymn Onward, Christian Soldiers, with words by Sabine Baring-Gould. The Salvation Army adopted it and it has become one of Britain's best loved hymns.

Gilbert & Sullivan – The Collaboration Begins

In 1871, John Hollingshead commissioned Gilbert to work with Sullivan on a holiday piece for Christmas, entitled Thespis, or The Gods Grown Old, at the Gaiety Theatre. It was a success and its run was extended beyond the length of the Gaiety's normal run. And that seemed to be that.

Gilbert and Sullivan now went their separate ways. Gilbert worked again with Clay on Happy Arcadia (1872), and with Alfred Cellier on Topsyturveydom (1874), as well as several farces, operetta libretti, extravaganzas, fairy comedies, adaptations from novels, translations from the French. In 1874, he published his last piece for Fun magazine ("Rosencrantz and Guildenstern"), almost three years after his last and then promptly resigned citing disapproval of the new owner's other publishing interests.

Sullivan was busy on large-scale works in the early 1870s with the Festival Te Deum (Crystal Palace, 1872); and the oratorio, The Light of the World (Birmingham Festival, 1873). He also wrote suites of incidental music for productions of The Merry Wives of Windsor at the Gaiety in 1874 and Henry VIII at the Theatre Royal, Manchester in 1877 as well as continuing composing hymns.

In 1873, Sullivan had also contributed songs to Burnand's Christmas "drawing room extravaganza", The Miller and His Man.

By 1875 conditions were right for Gilbert and Sullivan to work together again. Back in 1868, Gilbert had published a short comedic libretto in Fun magazine entitled "Trial by Jury: An Operetta". In 1873, Gilbert had arranged with theatrical manager and composer, Carl Rosa, to expand this work into a one-act libretto. It was arranged that Rosa's wife was to sing the role of the plaintiff. Tragically, Rosa's wife died in childbirth in 1874. Gilbert offered the libretto to Richard D'Oyly Carte, but Carte could not use the piece at that time.

The project seemed grounded. A few months later Carte, was managing the Royalty Theatre, needed a short piece to pair with Offenbach's La Périchole. Carte had previously conducted Sullivan's Cox and Box and remembering that Gilbert had suggested a libretto to him, he reunited Gilbert and Sullivan. The result was the one-act comic opera Trial by Jury. Starring Sullivan's brother Fred as the Learned Judge, it became a surprise hit, as well as earning lavish praise from the critics. It played for over 300 performances in its first few seasons.

A short time after Trial had opened Sullivan wrote The Zoo, another one-act comic opera, with a libretto by B. C. Stephenson. It did not perform well. Now the path was clear for Gilbert & Sullivan to reteam together in earnest and dominate light opera for the next 15 years.

Light opera was not considered of much worth by serious critics. Gilbert wanted greater respect for himself and his profession. At that time plays were not published in a form suitable for a "gentleman's library", they were in the main cheap and unattractive in their look designed mainly for use by actors rather than the home reader. Gilbert now arranged in late 1875 for the publishers Chatto and Windus to print a volume of his plays in a format designed to appeal to the general reader, with an attractive binding and clear type, containing Gilbert's most respectable plays, including his most serious works, and mischievously capped off with Trial by Jury.

After the success of Trial by Jury, there were discussions towards reviving Thespis, but Gilbert and Sullivan were not able to agree on terms with Carte and his backers. The score to Thespis was never published, and tragically most of the music is now lost.

Carte took some time to gather together funds for another opera, and in this gap the ever-busy Gilbert produced several works including Tom Cobb (1875), Eyes and No Eyes (1875), and Princess Toto (1876), his last and most ambitious work with Clay, a three-act comic opera with full orchestra. He also found time to write two serious works, Broken Hearts (1875) and Dan'l Druce, Blacksmith (1876) and his most successful comic play, Engaged (1877), which inspired Oscar Wilde's The Importance of Being Earnest.

It was only by 1877 that Carte finally assembled enough investors to form the Comedy Opera Company with a mandate to launch a series of original English comic operas, beginning with a third collaboration between Gilbert and Sullivan, The Sorcerer, in November 1877.

The Sorcerer (1877), ran for 178 performances, a success by the standards of the day, but H.M.S. Pinafore (1878), which followed it, turned Gilbert and Sullivan into an international phenomenon. The bright and cheerful music of Pinafore was composed during a time when Sullivan was in the middle of a health scare. He was in terrible pain from a kidney stone. H.M.S. Pinafore ran for 571 performances in London, the then-second-longest theatrical run in history, it also gave birth to and more than 150 unauthorised productions in America alone. Although this increased the reach of their reputations it added nothing to their profits.

It was noted in the Times review of H.M.S. Pinafore that the opera was an early attempt at the establishment of a "national musical stage" ... free from risqué French "improprieties" and without the "aid" of Italian and German musical models.

As the profits rolled in came acrimony among the investors who felt the shares were unequal. One night the other Comedy Opera Company partners hired thugs to storm the theatre to steal the sets and costumes in order that they could mount a rival production. This was beaten off by stagehands and others at the theatre loyal to Carte. Carte was to now continue as sole impresario of the newly renamed D'Oyly Carte Opera Company.

For the next decade, the Savoy Operas were Gilbert's principal activity. The successful comic operas with Sullivan continued to appear every year or two, several of them being among the longest-running productions of the musical stage. After Pinafore came The Pirates of Penzance (1879), Patience (1881), Iolanthe (1882), Princess Ida (1884 and based on Gilbert's earlier farce, The Princess), The Mikado (1885), Ruddigore (1887), The Yeomen of the Guard (1888), and The Gondoliers (1889). Gilbert not only directed and oversaw all aspects of production, but he designed the costumes himself for Patience, Iolanthe, Princess Ida, and Ruddigore. He insisted on precise and authentic sets and costumes, which provided a foundation to ground and focus his absurd characters and situations.

In 1878, Gilbert realised a lifelong dream to play Harlequin, which he did at the Gaiety Theatre in an amateur charity production of The Forty Thieves, written partly by himself. Gilbert trained for Harlequin's stylised dancing with his friend John D'Auban, who had arranged the dances for some of his plays and would choreograph most of the Gilbert and Sullivan operas. Producer John Hollingshead later remembered, "the gem of the performance was the grimly earnest and determined Harlequin of W. S. Gilbert. It gave me an idea of what Oliver Cromwell would have made of the character."

In 1879, Sullivan suggested to a reporter from The New York Times the secret of his success with Gilbert: "His ideas are as suggestive for music as they are quaint and laughable. His numbers ... always give me musical ideas."

During this time, Gilbert and Sullivan also collaborated on one other major work. In 1880, Sullivan was appointed director of the triennial Leeds Music Festival. For his first festival he was commissioned to write a sacred choral work. He chose Henry Hart Milman's 1822 dramatic poem based on the life and death of Saint Margaret the Virgin for its basis. It premiered at the Leeds music festival in October 1880. Gilbert arranged the original epic poem by Henry Hart Milman into a libretto suitable for the music.

Carte opened the next Gilbert and Sullivan piece, Patience, in April 1881 at London's Opera Comique, where their past three operas had played. In October, Patience transferred to the new, larger, state-of-the-art (it was the first theatre to be lit entirely with electricity) Savoy Theatre, built with the profits of the previous Gilbert and Sullivan works.

From now on all of the partnership's collaborations were produced at the Savoy. The first to actually premiere here was Iolanthe in 1882, it was their fourth hit in a row.

Cracks were beginning to surface between the partners. Sullivan, despite the financial security, began to view his work with Gilbert as beneath his skills, as well as being repetitious. After Iolanthe, Sullivan had not intended to write a new work with Gilbert, but when his broker went bankrupt in late 1882 he suffered serious financial loss. Needs must and Sullivan buckled down to continue writing Savoy operas. In February 1883, he and Gilbert signed a five-year agreement with Carte, requiring them to produce a new comic opera on six months' notice.

The ever watchful Gilbert had the previous year installed a telephone in his home and another at the prompt desk at the Savoy Theatre, so that he could listen in on performances and rehearsals from his home study. Gilbert had referred to the new technology in Pinafore in 1878, only two years after the device was invented and before London even had telephones.

Better news arrived for Sullivan on May 22nd, 1883, when he was knighted by Queen Victoria for his "services ... rendered to the promotion of the art of music" in Britain. The musical establishment, and many critics, believed that this would put an end to his career as a composer of comic opera – that a musical knight should not stoop below oratorio or grand opera. But Sullivan having just signed the five-year agreement and the financial security that gave him could no nothing to change course now.

The next opera, Princess Ida in 1884, which was the duo's only three-act, blank verse work, stuttered. Its run was much shorter. Sullivan's score was praised but with box office receipts lagging in March 1884, Carte gave the six months' notice, under the partnership contract, requiring a new opera.

Sullivan's friend, composer Frederic Clay, had suffered a serious stroke in early December 1883 that ended his career at only 45 years of age. Sullivan, with his own longstanding kidney problems, and his desire to devote himself to more serious music, replied to Carte, "It is impossible for me to do another piece of the character of those already written by Gilbert and myself."

Gilbert however was already at work on it. His idea revolved around a plot in which people fell in love against their wills after taking a magic lozenge. Sullivan was unequoviacal in his response. On April 1st, 1884 he wrote that he had "come to the end of my tether with the operas. I have been continually keeping down the music in order that not one syllable should be lost.... I should like to set a story of human interest & probability where the humorous words would come in a humorous not serious situation, & where, if the situation were a tender or dramatic one the words would be of similar character."

There was now a lengthy exchange of correspondence in which Sullivan called Gilbert's plot sketch (particularly the "lozenge" element) unacceptably mechanical, and too similar in both its grotesque "elements of topsyturveydom" and in actual plot to their earlier work, especially The Sorcerer, and requested, time and again, that a new subject be found.

This impasse was finally resolved on May 8th when Gilbert proposed a plot that would be their most successful: The Mikado (1885). It was to run for a staggering 672 performances.

In 1886, Sullivan composed his last large-scale choral work of the decade. It was a cantata for the Leeds Festival, The Golden Legend, based on Longfellow's poem of the same name. Apart from the comic operas, this proved to be Sullivan's best received full-length work. It was given hundreds of performances during his lifetime alone.

Ruddigore followed The Mikado in 1887. It was profitable, but its nine-month run was deemed to be disappointing compared with the earlier Savoy operas.

Gilbert was always keen to use a good idea again and proposed for their next piece another version of the magic lozenge plot. It was immediately rejected by Sullivan. Gilbert finally proposed a quite serious opera, to which Sullivan was in agreement. Although not a grand opera, The Yeomen of the Guard (1888) gave him the opportunity to compose his most ambitious stage work to date. In 1885, Sullivan had told an interviewer, ""The opera of the future is a compromise (among the French, German and Italian schools) – a sort of eclectic school, a selection of the merits of each one. I myself will make an attempt to produce a grand opera of this new school. ... Yes, it will be an historical work, and it is the dream of my life."

After The Yeomen of the Guard opened, Sullivan turned once again to Shakespeare and composed incidental music for Henry Irving's production of Macbeth (1888).

Sullivan wished to produce further serious works with Gilbert. He had collaborated with no other librettist since 1875. Gilbert felt the reaction to The Yeomen of the Guard had "not been so convincing as to warrant us in assuming that the public want something more earnest still." Gilbert countered by proposing that Sullivan should go ahead with his plan to write a grand opera, as well as comic works for the Savoy. Sullivan was not immediately persuaded. He replied, "I have lost the liking for writing comic opera, and entertain very grave doubts as to my power of doing it."

Nevertheless, Sullivan soon commissioned a grand opera libretto from Julian Sturgis (the recommendation came from Gilbert), while suggesting to Gilbert that he revive an old idea for an opera set in colourful Venice. The comic opera was completed first in 1889. The Gondoliers has been described as a pinnacle of Sullivan's achievement. It was to be the last great Gilbert and Sullivan success.

In April 1890, during the run of The Gondoliers, Gilbert objected to Carte's financial accounts which included a charge to the partnership for the cost of new carpeting for the Savoy Theatre lobby. Gilbert believed that this was a maintenance expense that should be charged to Carte alone. Carte who was building a new theatre to present Sullivan's forthcoming grand opera was adamant that it was legitimate. Sullivan sided with Carte, even going so far as to testify erroneously as to certain old debts.

The partners were in fundamental disagreement and the relationship was for all intents and purposes ruptured.

Gilbert took legal action against Carte and Sullivan and refused to write a word more for the Savoy. Sullivan wrote to Gilbert in September 1890 that he was "physically and mentally ill over this wretched business. I have not yet got over the shock of seeing our names coupled ... in hostile antagonism over a few miserable pounds".

From Gilbert's point of view Carte had either made a series of serious blunders in the accounts, or deliberately attempted to swindle his partners.

Gilbert wrote to Sullivan on May 28th, 1891, a year after the end of the "Quarrel", that Carte had admitted "an unintentional overcharge of nearly £1,000 in the electric lighting accounts alone." It seemed to illustrate Gilbert's point.

Work beckoned for Gilbert and he got on with it. He wrote The Mountebanks with Alfred Cellier and then a flop Haste to the Wedding with George Grossmith. Sullivan wrote Haddon Hall with Sydney Grundy.

In the Courts Gilbert prevailed in the lawsuit and felt vindicated. Although there was acrimony and bitterness between them the partnership had been so profitable that, after the financial failure of the Royal English Opera House, Carte and his wife sought to reunite the author and composer.

In 1891, after numerous failed attempts at a reconciliation, Tom Chappell, the music publisher who printed the Gilbert and Sullivan operas, stepped in to mediate between his two most profitable artists, and within two weeks, against the odds, had succeeded. The result was to be two more operas: Utopia, Limited (1893) and The Grand Duke (1896).

A third was almost achieved when Gilbert offered a third libretto to Sullivan (His Excellency, 1894), but his insistence on casting Nancy McIntosh, his protegée from Utopia, led to Sullivan's refusal.

Utopia, was only a modest success, and The Grand Duke, in which a theatrical troupe, by means of a "statutory duel" and a conspiracy, takes political control of a grand duchy, was a failure.

The partnership now ended for good.

Graciously Gilbert would late write, "... Savoy opera was snuffed out by the deplorable death of my distinguished collaborator, Sir Arthur Sullivan. When that event occurred, I saw no one with whom I felt that I could work with satisfaction and success, and so I discontinued to write libretti."

WS Gilbert – Life After the Partnership

In 1889 Gilbert financed the building of the Garrick Theatre. The following year the Gilberts moved to Grim's Dyke in Harrow. In 1891, Gilbert was appointed Justice of the Peace for Middlesex. After casting Nancy McIntosh in Utopia, Limited, he and Lady Gilbert developed an affection for her, and she eventually gained the status of an unofficially adopted daughter, moving to Grim's Dyke to live with them. She continued living there, even after Gilbert's death, until Lady Gilbert's death in 1936.

Although Gilbert announced a retirement from the theatre after the poor initial run of his last work with Sullivan, The Grand Duke (1896) and the poor reception of his 1897 play The Fortune Hunter, he produced at least three more plays over the last dozen years of his life, including an unsuccessful opera, Fallen Fairies (1909), with Edward German.

Gilbert, as we know was very keen on keeping his plays in the shape they were originally intended and continued to supervise the various revivals of his works by the D'Oyly Carte Opera Company, including its London Repertory seasons in 1906–09.

The last play he wrote, The Hooligan, produced just four months before his death, is a study of a young condemned thug in a prison cell. Gilbert shows sympathy for his protagonist, the son of a thief who, brought up among thieves, kills his girlfriend.

This grim, yet powerful piece, became one of Gilbert's most successful serious dramas, and it is easy to see why many thought he was developing a new style only for death to rob of us of what would surely be a fascinating journey.

In these last years, Gilbert wrote children's book versions of H.M.S. Pinafore and The Mikado giving, in some cases, backstory that is not found in the librettos.

Official recognition for him came on July 15th, 1907 with his knighthood in recognition of his contributions to drama. Gilbert was the first British writer ever to receive a knighthood for his plays alone—earlier dramatist knights were knighted for political and other services.

On May 29th, 1911, Gilbert was about to give a swimming lesson to Winifred Isabel Emery and 17-year-old Ruby Preece in the lake of his home, Grim's Dyke, when Preece lost her footing and called for help. Gilbert dived in to save her but suffered a heart attack in the middle of the lake and died.

William Schwenck was cremated at Golders Green and his ashes buried at the Church of St. John the Evangelist, Stanmore. The inscription on Gilbert's memorial on the south wall of the Thames Embankment in London reads: "His Foe was Folly, and his Weapon Wit".

George Grossmith wrote to The Daily Telegraph that, although Gilbert had been described as an autocrat at rehearsals, "That was really only his manner when he was playing the part of stage director at rehearsals. As a matter of fact, he was a generous, kind true gentleman, and I use the word in the purest and original sense."

Gilbert's legacy, aside from building the Garrick Theatre are the canon of Savoy Operas and other works that are either still being performed or in print all these years later. He has made a lasting and defining influence on both the American and British musical theatre. The innovations in content and form of the works that he and Sullivan developed, and in Gilbert's theories of acting and stage direction, directly influenced the development of the modern musical throughout the 20th century. Gilbert's lyrics use punning, as well as complex internal and two and three-syllable rhyme schemes, and served as a model for such 20th century Broadway lyricists as P.G. Wodehouse, Cole Porter, Ira Gershwin, and Lorenz Hart.

Gilbert's influence on the English language has also been marked, with well-known phrases such as "A policeman's lot is not a happy one", "short, sharp shock", "What never? Well, hardly ever!", and "let the punishment fit the crime" arising from his pen.

Arthur Sullivan – Life After the Partnership

Sullivan's only grand opera, Ivanhoe, based on Walter Scott's novel, opened at Carte's new Royal English Opera House on January 31st, 1891. Sullivan completed the score too late to meet Carte's planned production date, and costs had overrun to such an extent that Carte insisted on a contractual penalty of

£3,000 for the delay. However, when it opened it ran 155 consecutive performances, a wonderful run for a serious opera, and garnered good reviews. Afterwards, Carte was unable to fill the new opera house with other productions, and, unfairly, Ivanhoe was blamed for the failure of the opera house.

Later in 1891, New York beckoned for Sullivan and his music for Tennyson's The Foresters, which ran at Daly's Theatre in New York in 1892, but failed in London the following year.

Sullivan returned to comic opera, but needed a new collaborator. His next piece was Haddon Hall in 1892, with a libretto by Sydney Grundy based somewhat loosely on the elopement of Dorothy Vernon with John Manners. Although still comic, the tone and style of the work was more serious and romantic than the operas with Gilbert. It nonetheless enjoyed a run of 204 performances, and earned critical praise.

In 1894 Sullivan teamed up again with F. C. Burnand for The Chieftain, a heavily-reworked version of their earlier two-act opera, The Contrabandista, alas it failed.

The following year Sullivan provided incidental music for the Lyceum, this time for J. Comyns Carr's King Arthur.

As we know Gilbert and Sullivan did reunite for The Grand Duke in 1896. But it failed and they never worked together again. This did not affect the constant revival of their earlier operas at the Savoy.

In May 1897, Sullivan's full-length ballet, Victoria and Merrie England, opened at the Alhambra Theatre in celebration of the Queen's Diamond Jubilee. The work's seven scenes celebrate English history and culture, with the Victorian period as the grand finale. It ran for six months which was a great achievement. Following this was The Beauty Stone in 1898, with a libretto by Arthur Wing Pinero and J. Comyns Carr. Based on mediaeval morality plays the opera was a critical failure and, on the whole, a commercial failure running for only seven weeks.

Success came in 1899, to benefit "the wives and children of soldiers and sailors" on active service in the Boer War, when Sullivan composed the music of a jingoistic song, "The Absent-Minded Beggar", to a text by Rudyard Kipling. It was a sensation and raised a staggering £250,000 from performances and the sale of sheet music and other merchandise. Later that year he returned to his comic roots with In The Rose of Persia, with a libretto by Basil Hood overlapping a setting of exotic Arabian Nights with plot elements of The Mikado. It was well received, and, apart from those with Gilbert, was his most successful full-length collaboration. Another opera with Hood, The Emerald Isle, quickly went into preparation, but sadly Sullivan died before it completion.

On November 22nd, 1900 Arthur Seymour Sullivan died of heart failure, following an attack of bronchitis, at his flat in London. The unfinished opera, The Emerald Isle, was completed by Edward German and premiered in 1901. His Te Deum Laudamus, written to commemorate the end of the Boer War, was performed posthumously.

Sullivan wished to be buried in Brompton Cemetery with his parents and brother, but by order of the Queen he was buried in St. Paul's Cathedral. In addition to his knighthood, honours awarded to Sullivan in his lifetime included Doctor in Music, honoris causa, by the universities of Cambridge (1876) and Oxford (1879); Chevalier, Légion d'honneur, France (1878); The Order of the Medjidieh conferred by the

Sultan of Turkey (1888); and appointment as a Member of the Fourth Class of the Royal Victorian Order (MVO) in 1897.

In all, Sullivan's artistic output included 23 operas, 13 major orchestral works, eight choral works and oratorios, two ballets, one song cycle, incidental music to several plays, numerous hymns and other church pieces, and a large body of songs, parlour ballads, part songs, carols, and piano and chamber pieces.

Although Sullivan had several long term affairs and was also known to have a roving eye that led him to frequent liaisons with many other women he never married.

Rachel Scott Russell was the first of his great loves. Her parents' disapproval meant they met secretly but by 1868, Sullivan was enmeshed in a simultaneous and secret affair with Rachel's sister Louise. Both relationships had ceased by early 1869.

Sullivan's affair with the American socialite, Fanny Ronalds, a woman three years his senior, who had two children began when they met in Paris around 1867. The affair began in earnest soon after she moved to London in 1871. Despite his wandering ways she was a constant companion up to the time of Sullivan's death, but around 1889 or 1890, the sexual relationship seems to have ended.

In 1896, the 54-year-old Sullivan proposed marriage to 22-year-old Violet Beddington but she refused.

The favourite playgrounds for Sullivan were Paris and the south of France, with friends ranging from European royalty to Claude Debussy, and where the casinos enabled him to indulge his passion for gambling.

Sullivan enjoyed playing tennis although, according to George Grossmith, "I have seen some bad lawn-tennis players in my time, but I never saw anyone so bad as Arthur Sullivan".

He was devoted to his parents, particularly his mother, until her death in 1882. Henry Lytton wrote, "I believe there was never a more affectionate tie than that which existed between Sullivan and his mother, a very witty old lady, and one who took an exceptional pride in her son's accomplishments.

Sullivan once explained his method of working; "I don't use the piano in composition – that would limit me terribly". Sullivan explained that he did not wait for inspiration, but had "to dig for it. ... I decide on the rhythm before I come to the question of melody. ... I mark out the metre in dots and dashes, and not until I have quite settled on the rhythm do I proceed to actual notation."

In composing the Savoy operas, Sullivan wrote the vocal lines of the musical numbers first, and these were given to the actors. He, or an assistant, improvised a piano accompaniment at the early rehearsals; he wrote the orchestrations later, after he had seen what Gilbert's stage business would be. He left the overtures until last and often delegated their composition, based on his outlines, to his assistants, often adding his suggestions or corrections. Those Sullivan wrote himself include Thespis, Iolanthe, Princess Ida, The Yeomen of the Guard, The Gondoliers, The Grand Duke and probably Utopia Limited. Most of the overtures are structured as a potpourri of tunes from the operas in three sections: fast, slow and fast. The overtures from the Gilbert and Sullivan operas remain popular. Sullivan invariably conducted the operas on their opening nights.

In general, Sullivan preferred to write in major keys. In the Savoy operas less than 5% of the numbers are in a minor key and even in his serious works the major prevails. Sullivan was happy on occasion to use chords traditionally considered technically incorrect. When reproached for using consecutive fifths in Cox and Box, he replied "if 5ths turn up it doesn't matter, so long as there is no offence to the ear."

Sullivan's orchestra for the Savoy Operas was typical of any other pit orchestra of his era: 2 flutes (+ piccolo), oboe, 2 clarinets, bassoon, 2 horns, 2 cornets, 2 trombones, timpani, percussion and strings. According to Geoffrey Toye, the number of players in the Savoy orchestra was originally 31. Sullivan argued hard for an increase in the pit orchestra's size, and starting with The Yeomen of the Guard, the orchestra was augmented with a second bassoon and a bass trombone. Sullivan generally orchestrated each score at almost the last moment, noting that the accompaniment for an opera had to wait until he saw the staging, so that he could judge how heavily or lightly to orchestrate each part of the music. For his large-scale orchestral pieces, Sullivan added a second oboe part, sometimes double bassoon and bass clarinet, more horns, trumpets, tuba, and sometimes an organ and/or a harp. Many of these pieces used very large orchestras.

Sullivan's critical reputation has undergone extreme changes since he first came to prominence in the 1860s. At first, critics were struck by his potential, and he was hailed as the long-awaited great English composer. His incidental music to The Tempest received an acclaimed premiere at the Crystal Palace just before Sullivan's 20th birthday in April 1862. The Athenaeum wrote:

When Sullivan turned to comic opera with Gilbert, the serious critics began to express disapproval. Peter Gammond writes of "misapprehensions and prejudices, delivered to our door by the Victorian firm Musical Snobs Ltd. ... frivolity and high spirits were sincerely seen as elements that could not be exhibited by anyone who was to be admitted to the sanctified society of Art." As early as 1877 The Figaro wrote that Sullivan "has all the ability to make him a great composer, but he wilfully throws his opportunity away. ... He possesses all the natural ability to have given us an English opera, and, instead, he affords us a little more-or-less excellent fooling." Few critics denied the excellence of Sullivan's theatre scores. The Theatre wrote that "Iolanthe sustains Dr Sullivan's reputation as the most spontaneous, fertile, and scholarly composer of comic opera this country has ever produced." However, comic opera, no matter how skilfully crafted, was viewed as an intrinsically lower form of art than oratorio. The Athenaeum's review of The Martyr of Antioch declared: "It is an advantage to have the composer of H.M.S. Pinafore occupying himself with a worthier form of art."

Although the more solemn members of the musical establishment could not forgive Sullivan for writing music that was both comic and accessible, he was, nevertheless, "the nation's de facto composer laureate".

Gilbert & Sullivan – A Concise Bibliography

The Collaborative Pieces

All of these operas are full-length two-act works, except for Trial by Jury, which is in one act, and Princess Ida, which is three acts.

Thespis (1871)

Trial by Jury (1875)
The Sorcerer (1877)
H.M.S. Pinafore (1878)
The Pirates of Penzance (1879)
Patience (1881)
Iolanthe (1882)
Princess Ida (1884)
The Mikado (1885)
Ruddigore (1887)
The Yeomen of the Guard (1888)
The Gondoliers (1889)
Utopia, Limited (1893)
The Grand Duke (1896)

W.S. Gilbert – his Other Works

Poetry
The Bab Ballads, a collection of comic verse published roughly between 1865 and 1871
Songs of a Savoyard, London, 1890, a collection of Gilbert's song lyrics.

Short Stories
Foggerty's Fairy & Other Tales, a collection of short stories and essays, mainly from before 1874.

Some other short stories but not in the above appear here:-

Belgravia, Vol. 2 (1867). "From St. Paul's to Piccadilly," pp. 67–74
Fun, Vol. 1 new series (1865-1866) (several contributions by Gilbert; near end of volume)
Fun Christmas Number 1865, ("The Astounding Adventure of Wheeler J. Calamity,")
London Society, Vol. 13 (1868) (three "Thumbnail Sketches" by Gilbert)
On the Cards: Routledge's Christmas Annual (1867) ("Diamonds," and "The Converted Clown,")

Other Books
The Pinafore Picture Book, 1908, retelling the story of H.M.S. Pinafore for children, in prose narrative
The Story of The Mikado, 1921, a similar retelling of The Mikado for children

Plays and Musical Stage Works
Selected stage works that were important to Gilbert's career or were otherwise notable, in chronological order, excluding those listed under other headings below:

Dulcamara, or the Little Duck and the Great Quack (1866)
La Vivandière (1867)
Harlequin Cock Robin and Jenny Wren (1867), a Christmas pantomime.
The Merry Zingara (1868)

Robert the Devil (1868), it opened the Gaiety Theatre, London and ran in the provinces for 3 years.
The Pretty Druidess (1869), a parody of Norma – the last of Gilbert's five "operatic burlesques"
An Old Score (1869) (rewritten as "Quits!" in 1872) Gilbert's first full-length comedy.
The Princess (1870). Musical farce; the precursor to Princess Ida.
The Palace of Truth (1870).
Creatures of Impulse (1871), music by Alberto Randegger. From Gilberts story "A Strange Old Lady".
Pygmalion and Galatea (1871).
Randall's Thumb (1871). A comedy that opened the Royal Court Theatre.
The Wicked World (1873).
The Happy Land (1873). This work was briefly banned for its sharp satire of government ministers.
The Realm of Joy (1873).
The Wedding March (1873) a farce adapted from Un Chapeau de Paille d'Italie.
Rosencrantz & Guildenstern (published 1874, performed 1891). Gilbert's burlesque of Hamlet.
Charity (1874). Concerns Victorian attitudes towards sex outside of marriage.
Sweethearts (1874).
Tom Cobb (1875).
Broken Hearts (1875). The last of Gilbert's "fairy comedies", this was one of Gilbert's favourite plays.
Dan'l Druce, Blacksmith (1876).
Engaged (1877).
The Ne'er-do-Weel (1878); rewritten as "The Vagabond" after a few weeks.
The Forty Thieves (1878). Co-written with three other writers, WSG played Harlequin.
Gretchen (1879)
Foggerty's Fairy (1881)
Brantinghame Hall (1888) Gilbert's biggest flop, it sent producer Rutland Barrington into bankruptcy.
The Fortune Hunter (1897). Its reception provoked WSG to announce retiring from writing for the stage.
The Fairy's Dilemma (1904).
The Hooligan (1911).

German Reed Entertainments

Gilbert wrote six one-act musical entertainments for the German Reeds between 1869 and 1875. They were successful in their own right and also helped form Gilbert's mature style as a dramatist.

No Cards (1869)
Ages Ago (1869). Gilbert's first collaboration with Frederic Clay, ran for 350 performances.
Our Island Home (1870)
A Sensation Novel (1871)
Happy Arcadia (1872)
Eyes and No Eyes (1875)

Early Comic Operas

The Gentleman in Black (1870; music by Frederic Clay). The score is lost.
Les Brigands (1871), an English adaptation of Jacques Offenbach's operetta.
Topsyturveydom (1874; music by Alfred Cellier). The score is lost.
Princess Toto (1876; music by Frederic Clay). A three-act opera.

Later Operas (Without Sullivan)
Though not as popular as the works with Arthur Sullivan, a few of Gilbert's later works arguably have stronger plots than the last two Gilbert and Sullivan operas.

The Mountebanks (1892; music; Alfred Cellier). This is the "lozenge plot" that Sullivan declined to set on several occasions.
Haste to the Wedding (1892; music; George Grossmith). An unsuccessful adaptation of The Wedding March.
His Excellency (1894; music; Osmond Carr). Gilbert felt that if Sullivan had set it, the piece would have been "another Mikado".
Fallen Fairies (1909; music by Edward German). Gilbert's last opera, which was a failure.

Parlour Ballads
The Yarn of the Nancy Bell, with music by Alfred Plumpton. One of the Bab Ballads. 1869.
Thady O'Flynn, with music by James L. Molloy. 1868. From No Cards.
Would You Know that Maiden Fair, with music by Frederic Clay. From Ages Ago. c. 1869.
Corisande, with music by James L. Molloy. 1870.
Eily's Reason, with music by James L. Molloy. 1871.
Three songs from A Sensation Novel: "The Detective's Song", "The Tyrannical Bridegroom", and "The Jewel". 1871
The Distant Shore, with music by Arthur Sullivan. 1874.
The Love that Loves me Not, with music by Arthur Sullivan. 1875.
Sweethearts, with music by Arthur Sullivan. 1875.
Let Me Stay, with music by Walter Maynard. 1875.

Arthur Sullivan – His Other Works

Operas
The Sapphire Necklace (ca. 1863; unperformed)
Cox and Box (1866)
The Contrabandista (1867)
The Zoo (1875)
Ivanhoe (1891)
Haddon Hall (1892)
The Chieftain (1894)
The Beauty Stone (1898)
The Rose of Persia (1899)
The Emerald Isle (1901; completed by Edward German)

Incidental Music to Plays
The Tempest (1861)
The Merchant of Venice (1871)
The Merry Wives of Windsor (1874)
Henry VIII (1877)

Macbeth (1888)
Tennyson's The Foresters (1892)
J. Comyns Carr's King Arthur for Henry Irving (1895)

Ballets and Song Cycle
L'Île Enchantée (1864 ballet)
Victoria and Merrie England (1897 ballet)
The Window; or, The Song of the Wrens (1871 song cycle)

Choral Works with Orchestra
The Masque at Kenilworth (1864)
The Prodigal Son (Sullivan) (1869)
On Shore and Sea (1871)
Festival Te Deum (1872)
The Light of the World (Sullivan) (1873)
The Martyr of Antioch (1880)
Ode for the Opening of the Colonial and Indian Exhibition (1886)
The Golden Legend (1886)
Ode for the Laying of the Foundation Stone of The Imperial Institute (1887)
Te Deum Laudamus (1902; performed posthumously)

Orchestral Works
Overture in D (1858; now lost)
Overture The Feast of Roses (1860; now lost)
Procession March (1863)
Princess of Wales's March (1863)
Symphony in E, "Irish" (1866)
Overture in C, "In Memoriam" (1866)
Concerto for Cello and Orchestra (1866)
Overture Marmion (1867)
Overture di Ballo (1870)
Imperial March (1893)
The Absent-Minded Beggar March (1899)

Other Works

Songs & Parlour Ballads
Absent-minded Beggar (Rudyard Kipling) 1899
Arabian Love Song (Percy Bysshe Shelley) 1866
Ay de mi, My Bird (George Eliot)1874
Bid me at least Goodbye (Sydney Grundy) 1894
Birds in the Night (Lionel H. Lewin) 1869

Bride from the North (Henry F. Chorley) 1863
Care is all Fiddle-dee-dee (F. C. Burnand) 1874
Chorister, The (Fred. E. Weatherly) 1876
Christmas Bells at Sea (C. L. Kenney) 1875
County Guy (Walter Scott) 1867
Distant Shore, The (W. S. Gilbert) 1874
Dove Song (William Brough) 1869
E tu nol sai - see You Sleep (G. Mazzucato) 1889
Edward Gray (Alfred Tennyson)(1880
Ever (Mrs Bloomfield Moore) 1887
First Departure - see The Chorister (Rev. E. Munroe) 1874
Give (Adelaide Anne Procter) 1867
Golden Days (Lionel H. Lewin)1872
Guinevere! (Lionel H. Lewin) 1872
I Heard the Nightingale (Rev. C. H. Townsend) 1863
I Wish to Tune my Quiv'ring Lyre (Anacreon; trans. Lord Byron) 1868
I Would I were a King (Victor Hugo; trans. A. Cockburn) 1878
Ich möchte hinaus es jauchzen (A. Corrodi) 1859
If Doughty Deeds (Robert Graham of Gartmore) 1866
In the Summers Long Ago (J. P. Douglas) 1867
Let Me Dream Again (B. C. Stephenson) 1875
Lied, mit Thränen halbgeschrieben (Eichendorff)1861
Life that Lives for You (Lionel H. Lewin) 1870
Little Darling Sleep Again (Cradle Song) (anon) 1874
Living Poems (H. W. Longfellow)1874
Longing for Home (Jean Ingelow) 1904
Looking Back (Louisa Gray)1870
Looking Forward (Louisa Gray) 1873
Lost Chord, The (Adelaide Anne Procter) 1877
Love that Loves Me Not, The (W. S. Gilbert) 1875
Maiden's Story, The (Emma Embury) 1867
Marquis de Mincepie, The (F. C. Burnand) 1874
Mary Morison (Robert Burns) 1874
Moon in Silent Brightness, The (Bishop Reginald Heber) 1868
Mother's Dream, The (Rev. W. Barnes) 1868
My Dear and Only Love (Marquis of Montrose) 1874
My Dearest Heart (anon) 1874
My Heart is like a Silent Lute (Benjamin Disraeli) 1904
My Love - see "There Sits a Bird in Yonder Tree
My Love Beyond the Sea - see "In the Summers Long Ago"
None but I Can Say (Lionel H. Lewin)1872
O Fair Dove, O Fond Dove (Jean Ingelow) 1868
O Israel (Hosea) 1855
O Mistress Mine (William Shakespeare) 1866
O Swallow, Swallow (Alfred Tennyson) 1900
Oh Sweet and Fair (A. F. C. K.) 1868
Oh! bella mia - see "Oh! Ma Charmante"
Oh! Ma Charmante (Victor Hugo) 1872

Old Love Letters (S. K. Cowen) 1879
Once Again (Lionel H. Lewin) 1872
Orpheus with his Lute (William Shakespeare) 1866
River, The (anon) 1875
Roads Should Blossom, The (anon) 1864
Rosalind (William Shakespeare) 1866
Sad Memories (C. J. Rowe) 1869
Sailor's Grave, The (H. F. Lyte) 1872
St. Agnes' Eve (Alfred Tennyson) 1879
Shadow, A. (Adelaide Anne Procter)1886
She is not Fair to Outward View (Hartley Coleridge) 1866
Sigh no More, Ladies (William Shakespeare) 1866
Sleep My Love, Sleep (R. Whyte Melville) 1874
Snow Lies White, The (Jean Ingelow) 1868
Sometimes (Lady Lindsay of Balcarres) 1877
Sweet Day So Cool (George Herbert) 1864
Sweet Dreamer - see "Oh! Ma Charmante"
Sweethearts (W. S. Gilbert) 1875
Tears, Idle Tears (Alfred Tennyson) 1900
Tender and True (Dinah Maria Mulock) 1874
There Sits a Bird on Yonder TreeRev. (C. H. Barham) 1873
Thou art Lost to Me (anon) 1865
Thou art Weary (Adelaide Anne Procter) 1874
Thou'rt Passing Hence (Felicia Hemans) 1875
To One in Paradise (Edgar Allan Poe) 1904
Troubadour, The (Walter Scott) 1869
Village Chimes, The (C. J. Rowe) 1870
Weary Lot is Thine, Fair Maid, A (Walter Scott) 1866
We've Ploughed our Land (anon)1875
When Thou Art Near (W. J. Stewart) 1877
White Plume, The - see "The Bride from the North"
Will He Come? (Adelaide A. Procter) 1865
Willow Song, The (William Shakespeare)1866
You Sleep (B. C. Stephenson) 1889

Hymns (Title & First Line)
Adoro Te - Saviour, again to Thy dear name we raise (Arranger)
All This Night - All this night bright angels sing
Angel Voices - Angel voices, ever singing
Audite Audientes me - I heard the voice of Jesus say
Bethlehem - While shepherd's watched their flocks (Arranger)
Bishopgarth - O King of Kings, Whose reign of old
Bolwell - Thou to whom the sick and dying
Carrow - My God, I thank Thee Who has made
Chapel Royal - O love that wilt not let me go
Christus - Show me not only Jesus dying
Clarence - Winter reigneth o'er the land

Coena Domini - Draw nigh, and take the body of the Lord
Come Unto Me - Come unto Me, ye weary (Arranger)
Constance - I've found a Friend; oh, such a Friend
Coronae - Crown Him, with many crowns
Courage, Brother - Courage, brother, do not stumble
Dominion Hymn - God bless our wide dominion
Dulce Sonans - Angel voices, ever singing
Ecclesia - The church has waited long
Ellers - Saviour, again to Thy dear name we raise (Arranger)
Evelyn - In the hour of my distress
Ever Faithful - Let us with a gladsome mind
Fatherland (St. Edmund) - I'm but a stranger here
Formosa (Falfield) - Love Divine, all love excelling
Fortunatus - Welcome, happy morning!
Golden Sheaves - To Thee, O Lord, our hearts we raise
Hanford - Jesu, my Saviour, look on me
Heber (Gennesareth) - When through the torn sail
Holy City - Sing Alleluia forth in duteous praise
Hushed was the Evening Hymn - Hushed was the evening hymn
Hymn of the Homeland - The homeland, the homeland
Lacrymae - Lord, in this Thy mercy's day
Leominster - A few more years shall roll (Arranger)
Light - Holy Spirit! Come in might! (Arranger)
Litany (1) - Jesu, life of those who die
Litany (2) - Jesu, we are far away
Long Home, The - Tender Shepherd, Thou hast still'd
Lux eoi - All is bright and cheeful round us
Lux in Tenebris - Lead, kindly Light
Lux Mundi - O Jesu, Thou art standing
Marlborough - O Strength and Stay, upholding all creation (Arranger)
Mount Zion - Rock of Ages, cleft for me
Nearer Home - For ever with the Lord (Arranger)
Noel - It came upon the midnight clear (Arranger)
Old 137th - Great King of nations, hear our prayer (Arranger)
Paradise - O Paradise!
Parting - With the sweet word of peace (Arranger)
Pilgrimage - From Egypt's bondage come
Promissio Patris - Our blest Redeemer, ere He breathed
Propior Deo - Nearer, my God, to Thee
Rest - Art thou weary, art thou languid
Resurrexit - Christ is risen!
Roseate Hues, The - The roseate hues of early dawn
Safe Home - Safe home, safe home in port
St. Ann - The Son of God goes forth to war (Arranger)
St. Francis - O Father, who hast created all
St. Gertrude - Onward, Christian soldiers
St. Kevin - Come, ye faithful, raise the strain
St. Lucian - Of Thy love some gracious token

St. Luke (St. Nathaniel) - God moves in a mysterious way
St. Mary Magdalene - Saviour, when in dust to Thee
St. Millicent - Let no tears to-day be shed
St. Patrick - He is gone - a cloud of light
St. Theresa - Brightly gleams our banner
Saints of God - The Saints of God, their conflict past.
Springtime - For all Thy love and goodness (Arranger)
Strain Upraise, The - The Strain upraise in joy and praise
Thou God of Love - Thou God of Love, beneath Thy sheltering wing
Ultor Omnipotens - God the all terrible! King who ordainest
Valete - Sweet Saviour, bless us 'ere we go
Veni, Creator - Come Holy Ghost, our souls inspire
Victoria - To mourn our dead we gather here

Part Songs

The term "Part Song" is more usually applied to one where the highest part carries the melody with the other voices supplying the accompanying harmonies.

Also included here are the soprano duet, The Sisters, and the trio Sullivan composed for the play Olivia by W. G. Wills, Morn, Happy Morn.

O Lady Dear (Madrigal) - Composed 1857, unpublished.
It was a Lover and his Lass - Words by Shakespeare. Performed at the Royal Academy of Music, 1857, unpublished.
Seaside Thoughts - Words by Bernard Bartram. Composed 1857. Published 1904.
The Last Night of the Year - Words by H. F. Chorley. Published 1863.
O Hush Thee, My Babie - Words by Walter Scott. Published 1867.
The Rainy Day - Words by H. W. Longfellow. Published 1867.
Evening - Words by Lord Houghton, after Goethe. Published 1868.
Parting Gleams - Words by Aubrey de Vere. Published 1868.
Echoes - Words by Thomas Moore. Published 1868.
The Long Day Closes - Words by H. F. Chorley. Published 1868.
Joy to the Victors - Words by Walter Scott. Published 1868
The Beleaguered - Words by H. F. Chorley. Published 1868.
It Came Upon the Midnight Clear - Words by E. H. Sears. Published 1871.
Lead, Kindly Light - Words by J. H. Newman. Published 1871.
Through Sorrows Path - Words by H. Kirke White. Published 1871.
Say, Watchman, What of the Night? - Words from Isaiah. Published 1871.
The Way is Long and Dreary - Words by Adelaide Anne Procter. Published 1871.
Morn, Happy Morn - Composed for the play, Olivia by W. G. Wills. Published 1878.
The Sisters - Words by Alfred Tennyson. Published 1881.
Wreaths for our Graves - Words by L. F. Massey. Published 1898.
Fair Daffodils - Words by Robert Herrick. Published 1904.

Church Songs

By the Waters of Babylon - Composed c. 1850. Unpublished.
Sing unto the Lord - Composed 1855. Unpublished.
Psalm 103 - Composed 1856. Unpublished.
We have heard with our ears
(i) Dedicated to Sir George Smart and performed at the Chapel Royal, January 1860.
(ii) Dedicated to Rev. Thomas Helmore. 1865.
O Love the Lord - Dedicated to John Goss. 1864.
Te Deum, Jubilate, Kyrie (in D major) 1866.
O God, Thou art Worthy - Composed for the wedding of Adrian Hope, 3 June 1867. Published in 1871.
O Taste and See - Dedicated to Rev. C. H. Haweis. 1867.
Rejoice in the Lord - Composed for the wedding of Rev. R. Brown-Borthwick, 16 April 1868.
Sing, O Heavens - Dedicated to Rev. F. C. Byng. 1869.
I Will Worship - Dedicated to Rev. F. Gore Ouseley. 1871.
Two Choruses adapted from Russian Church Music, 1874.
(i) Turn Thee Again
(ii) Mercy and Truth
I Will Mention Thy Loving-kindness - Dedicated to John Stainer. 1875.
I Will Sing of Thy Power. 1877.
Hearken Unto Me, My People. 1877.
Turn Thy Face. 1878.
Who is Like unto Thee - Dedicated to Walter Parratt. 1883.
I Will Lay Me Down in Peace - Composed 1868. Published only in 1910.

Christmas Carols & Songs

Advent
Hearken unto me, my people - An Anthem for Advent or General Use. Words from Isaiah. (1877)

Christmas Carols
All this night bright angels sing - Words by W. Austin. (1870)
I Sing the Birth - Words by Ben Jonson. (1868)
It Came Upon the Midnight Clear - Words by E. H. Sears.
Part Song for Soprano Solo and Choir (1871)
Hymn Tune "Noel" (1874)
Upon the Snow-clad Earth (1876)
While Shepherds Watched - Words by Nahum Tate (1874)
Hark! What Mean those Holy Voices? - Words by John Cawood (1883)

Songs
Christmas Bells at Sea - Words by Charles Kenney (1875)
Two songs from The Miller and His Man - A Christmas Drawing Room Entertainment. Words by F. C. Burnand (1874)
The Marquis de Mincepie
Care is all Fiddle-dee-dee
The Last Night of the Year - Part Song - Words by H. F. Chorley (1863)

Chamber Music & Solo Piano

Scherzo - Piano Solo, 1857, unpublished.

Capriccio No. 2 - Piano Solo (unfinished), 1857, unpublished.

String Quartet - Performed at Leipzig, May 1859. Published 2000

Romance in G minor - For string quartet, 1859. Published 1964.

Thoughts - Two pieces for piano solo, Published by Cramer, 1862.

An Idyll - For Cello and Piano. Composed in 1865 and Published 1899.

Allegro Risoluto - Piano solo, 1866. Published only in 1974

Berceuse - Based on the theme of Hushed was the Bacon from Cox and Box but with additional material.

Day Dreams - Six pieces for piano solo. 1867

Duo Concertante - Cello and piano. 1868

Twilight - Piano solo. 1868